# Remember This?

*People, Things and Events*

FROM **1962** TO THE **PRESENT DAY**

US EDITION

# Rewind, Replay, Remember

What can you remember before you turned six? If you're like most of us, not much: the comforting smell of a blanket or the rough texture of a sweater, perhaps. A mental snapshot of a parent arriving home late at night. A tingle of delight or the shadow of sorrow.

But as we grow out of childhood, our autobiographical and episodic memories—they're the ones hitched to significant events such as birthdays or leaving school—are created and filed more effectively, enabling us to piece them together at a later date. And the more we revisit those memories, the less likely we are to lose the key that unlocks them.

We assemble these fragments into a more-or-less coherent account of our lives—the one we tell to ourselves, our friends, our relatives. And while this one-of-a-kind biopic loses a little definition over the years, some episodes remain in glorious technicolor—although it's usually the most embarrassing incidents!

But this is one movie that's never quite complete. Have you ever had a memory spring back unbidden, triggered by something seemingly unrelated? This book is an attempt to discover those forgotten scenes using the events, sounds, and faces linked to the milestones in your life.

It's time to blow off the cobwebs and see how much you can remember!

# It Happened in 1962

The biggest event in the year is one that didn't make the front pages: you were born! Here are some of the national stories that people were talking about.

+ Centralia Mine catches fire (it's still burning)
+ LED light demonstrated
+ The Mashed Potato becomes a dance craze
+ Shortest acceptance speech given for an Oscar award (Patty Duke: "Thank you.")
+ With a name like Smuckers... slogan appears
+ Avis rent-a-car service starts to try harder
+ Cuban Missile Crisis captivates the world
+ Commercial communications satellite launched
+ John F. Kennedy serenaded by Marilyn Monroe on his birthday
+ John Glenn orbits the Earth
+ Actress Hedy Lamarr's Wifi invention implemented
+ Cesar Chavez founds the United Farm Workers union
+ Marilyn Monroe found dead (right)
+ Taco Bell opens for business
+ First video game invented (Spacewar!)
+ Dr. Frances Kelsey awarded for banning thalidomide
+ Wal-Mart starts selling for less
+ Black student registered at University of Mississippi
+ Nixon gives his "last press conference"
+ Consumer Bill of Rights proposed
+ Spiderman appears in comic pages
+ Navy SEALs formed
+ Columbus Day Storm strikes ("The Big Blow")

*Born this year:*
- Actor Tom Cruise
- Singer Jon Bon Jovi
- Actress Jodie Foster
- Actress Demi Moore

New York Yankees center fielder, Joe DiMaggio, was married to Marilyn Monroe in 1954; the union lasted just 9 months. But eight years later it was DiMaggio who claimed her body, kept those he blamed away from her funeral (right), and sent roses to her grave every few days for 20 years. "I'll finally get to see Marilyn," he is reported to have said shortly before he died in 1999.

# On the Bookshelf When You Were Small

The books of our childhood linger long in the memory. These are the children's classics, all published in your first ten years. Do you remember the stories? What about the covers?

| | |
|---|---|
| 1962 | A Wrinkle in Time by Madeleine L'Engle |
| 1962 | The Snowy Day by Ezra Jack Keats |
| 1962 | Mr. Rabbit and the Lovely Present by Charlotte Zolotow |
| 1963 | Where the Wild Things Are by Maurice Sendak |
| 1963 | Clifford the Big Red Dog by Norman Bridwell |
| 1964 | **The Giving Tree by Shel Silverstein** |
| | Is this the most controversial apple tree in literature? The Giving Tree is a story of love and regularly ranks as a parental favorite. But for some it's a tale of taking selfishly, not giving—definitely one to be left on the shelf. |
| 1964 | Charlie and the Chocolate Factory by Roald Dahl |
| 1964 | **Chitty-Chitty-Bang-Bang by Ian Fleming** |
| | Published after Fleming's death, the book was adapted for film four years later, produced by Albert R. Broccoli and co-written by Roald Dahl. |
| 1965 | Lyle, Lyle, Crocodile by Bernard Waber |
| 1965 | The Mouse and the Motorcycle by Beverly Cleary |
| 1966 | Amelia Bedelia and the Surprise Shower by Peggy Parish |
| 1966 | Up a Road Slowly by Irene Hunt |
| 1967 | Never Talk to Strangers by Irma Joyce |
| 1967 | The Black Pearl by Scott O'Dell |
| 1968 | Richard Scarry's Best Storybook Ever by Richard Scarry |
| 1968 | The Kitten Book by Jan Pfloog |
| 1968 | Corduroy by Don Freeman |
| 1969 | **The Very Hungry Caterpillar by Eric Carle** |
| | A tale inspired by a hole punch, this much-loved picture book has clocked up worldwide sales of 50 million. |
| 1970 | Sing Down the Moon by Scott O'Dell |
| 1970 | Frog and Toad Are Friends by Arnold Lobel |
| 1970 | Are You There, God? It's Me, Margaret. by Judy Blume |
| 1971 | The Monster at the End of This Book by Jon Stone |

# Around the World in Your Birth Year

Here are the events from outside the US that were big enough to make news back home in the year you were born. And you won't remember any of them!

- Burundi claims independence from Belgium
- Man shot on Berlin Wall, left to die
- Floods around Hamburg kill 300
- Jamaica becomes independent
- Britain and France develop the Concorde
- 300 people use a tunnel to escape Berlin
- France grants Algeria independence
- Train crash in Denmark kills 93
- Nehru becomes Indian PM
- Hundreds die in avalanche in Peru
- Brazil wins World Cup
- Rolling Stones perform in public
- Pope John XXIII excommunicates Castro
- Tokyo triple-train crash kills 160
- Gay Byrnes begins broadcasting
- Eichmann is hanged for war crimes
- Plane crashes in Paris
- Rwanda splits from Burundi and gains independence
- French Foreign Legion leaves Algeria
- Cuban Missile Crisis grips the world's attention
- Argentine woman crowned Miss Universe
- Soviets agree to send arms to Cuba
- East Germany restarts conscription
- Military coup overthrows government in Burma
- Algeria joins the Arab League

# Boys' Names When You Were Born

Once upon a time, popular names came… and stuck. (John hogged the top spot for 40 years, to 1924.) These are the most popular names when you were born.

**Michael**
For 44 years from 1954 onwards, Michael was the nation's most popular name. (There was one blip in 1960 when David came first.)

David
John
James
Robert
Mark
William
Richard
Thomas
Jeffrey
Scott
Steven
Joseph
Kevin
Charles
Timothy
Daniel
Kenneth
Paul
Brian
Gregory
Gary
Donald
Anthony
Ronald

**Rising and falling stars:**
Tom and Ronnie made their last appearance, while Jonathan made his first. Gregory peaked this year, in 21st place.

# Girls' Names When You Were Born

Mary held the crown in every year from 1880 to 1946–and again from 1953. But nothing lasts forever…

### Lisa

Lisa finally toppled Mary to take the top spot–and she'd stay there until 1969 (when she was usurped by Jennifer).

Mary
Susan
Karen
Linda
Patricia
Donna
Cynthia
Deborah
Sandra
Lori
Brenda
Pamela
Barbara
Debra
Kimberly
Sharon
Teresa
Nancy
Elizabeth
Laura
Julie
Tammy
Cheryl
Robin
Diane

### Rising and falling stars:

Sherri, Penny and Andrea graced the Top 100 for the first time; for Peggy and Betty it would be their last ever year in the spotlight.

# Things People Did When You Were Growing Up...

...that hardly anyone does now. Some of these we remember fondly; others are best left in the past!

- Help Mom make cookies using a cookie press
- Keep bread in a breadbox
- Can and preserve vegetables from your garden
- Listen to daytime soap operas on the radio
- Participate in Church fundraisers
- Watch endurance competitions like flagpole sitting and goldfish eating
- Build scooters from roller skates and scrap wood
- Bring a slide-rule to math class
- Take a Sunday drive out to the country
- Play leapfrog
- Live in a Sears Modern Home ordered from the Sears catalog
- Get a treat from the pharmacy soda fountain
- Camp in a "Hooverville" while looking for work
- Keep a thrift or kitchen garden
- Buy penny candy
- Buy goods from door-to-door salesmen
- Wear clothing made from flour sacks
- Collect marbles
- Join a dance marathon
- Listen to Amos n' Andy on the radio on weekend evenings
- Eat Water Pie
- "Window shop" downtown on Saturdays
- Pitch pennies
- Earn $30 a month plus food and shelter working for the Civilian Conservation Corps

# How Many of These Games Are Still Played?

The first half of the 20th century was the heyday for new board and card games launched to the US public. Many became firm family favorites and have been around ever since. Which ones did you play?

| | |
|---|---|
| 1925 | Pegity |
| 1925 | Playing for the Cup |
| 1927 | Hokum ("The game for a roomful") |
| 1920s | The Greyhound Racing Game |
| 1930 | Wahoo |
| 1932 | Finance |
| 1934 | Sorry! |
| 1935 | **Monopoly**<br>The game's origins lie with The Landlord's Game, patented in 1904 by Elizabeth Magie. (The anti-monopoly version—Prosperity—didn't catch on.) It was the first game with a never-ending path rather than a fixed start and finish. |
| 1935 | Easy Money |
| 1936 | The Amazing Adventures of Fibber McGee |
| 1937 | Meet the Missus |
| 1937 | Stock Ticker |
| 1938 | Scrabble |
| 1938 | Movie Millions |
| 1940 | Dig |
| 1940 | Prowl Car |
| 1942 | Sea Raider |
| 1943 | Chutes and Ladders |
| 1949 | **Clue**<br>Clue—or Cluedo, as it is known to most outside the USA—introduced us to a host of shady characters and grisly murder weapons. For years those included a piece of genuine lead pipe, now replaced on health grounds. |
| 1949 | **Candy Land**<br>This wholesome family racing game, invented on a polio ward, was the victim of something less savory nearly 50 years after its launch when an adult website claimed the domain name. Thankfully, the courts swiftly intervened. |

# Things People Do Now...

...that were virtually unknown when you were young. How many of these habits are part of your routine or even second nature these days? Do you remember the first time?

- Get curbside grocery pickup
- Stream movies instead of going to Blockbuster for a rental
- Learn remotely and online
- Communicate by text or video chat
- Use a Kindle or other e-reading device
- Go geocaching
- Track your sleep, exercise, or fertility with a watch
- Use a weighted blanket
- Use a robotic/automatic vacuum
- Take your dog to a dog park
- Have a package delivered by drone
- Find a date online or through an app
- Use hand sanitizer
- Automatically soothe your baby with a self-rocking bassinet
- Host a gender-reveal party during pregnancy
- Use a home essential oil diffuser or salt lamp
- Have a "destination wedding"
- Use a device charging station while waiting for a flight
- Get a ride from Uber or Lyft instead of a taxi
- Drink hard seltzer
- Take a home DNA test (for you... or your pet)
- Have a telemedicine/virtual healthcare visit
- Smoke an e-cigarette/"vape"
- Start your car, dryer, or air conditioner via an app

# Popular Food in the 1950s

The decade before you were born brought more of one thing in particular on the table: meat. In the yard, men stepped up to the barbeque to sharpen their skills. In the kitchen, fancy new electric appliances and frozen TV dinners promised convenience and new, exotic flavors. These fifties favorites became staples of the sixties, too.

Tuna noodle casserole

Dinty Moore Beef Stew

Beef stroganoff

**Green bean casserole**

Green bean casserole was invented in the Campbell's test kitchen in 1955 as a cheap, fuss-free dish. Today, around 40 percent of Campbell's Cream of Mushroom soup sold in the US goes into this dinner table staple.

**Pigs-in-a-blanket**

Pigs get different blankets in the United Kingdom, where sausages are wrapped in bacon rather than pastry.

Backyard barbecues

Ovaltine

Swedish meatballs

Pineapple upside down cake

**Spam**

Ground pork shoulder and ham sold in a distinctive can—for much of the world, that means Spam. This "meatloaf without basic training" is affordable and still popular, with over eight billion cans sold since it was first sold in 1937.

Ambrosia salad

Sugar Smacks

Cheez Whiz

Campbell's Tomato Soup spice cake

**Swanson Turkey TV Dinners**

Dreamed up as a solution to an over-supply of turkey, TV dinners proved nearly as popular as the TV itself. Swanson sold over 25 million of them in 1954, the year these handy meal packs were launched.

Veg-All canned vegetables

Chicken à la King

# Cars of your Childhood

Was the golden age of automobiles already behind you? As the sixties began, highways still thronged with cars sporting the Space Age theme of the fifties—sweeping lines, tailfins, and cascading chrome grilles.

| | |
|---|---|
| 1926 | Chrysler Imperial |
| 1936 | General Motors Buick Roadmaster |
| 1939 | **Studebaker Champion** |
| | Over seven decades, the Champion's creator, Raymond Loewy, designed railroads, logos, buses, vending machines, and a space station for NASA. |
| 1939 | Chrysler DeSoto Custom |
| 1947 | Studebaker Starlight Coupe |
| 1948 | **Crosley Station Wagon** |
| | The first car to be marketed as "Sports Utility." |
| 1948 | Jaguar XK120 |
| 1949 | **Muntz Jet** |
| | Fewer than 200 Muntz Jets were built by founder Madman Muntz, an engineer who married seven times and made (and lost) fortunes selling cars, TVs, and more. |
| 1949 | Chrysler Dodge Coronet |
| 1950 | General Motors Chevrolet Bel-Air |
| 1950 | Nash Rambler |
| 1951 | Hudson Hornet |
| 1953 | General Motors Chevrolet Corvette |
| 1953 | General Motors Buick Skylark |
| 1953 | General Motors Cadillac Eldorado |
| 1953 | Nash Metropolitan |
| 1954 | Ford Skyliner |
| 1955 | Ford Thunderbird |
| 1955 | Ford Fairlane |
| 1956 | Studebaker Golden Hawk |
| 1956 | Chrysler Plymouth Fury |
| 1957 | **Mercedes-Benz 300 SL Roadster** |
| | Voted "Sports Car of the Century" in 1999. |

Cars crawl out of 1950s Philadelphia over the Ben Franklin Bridge. Henry Ford wasn't the only one to "build a car for the great multitude." Millions of new suburbanites embraced their newfound freedom—even if that meant driving to the same place as everyone else.

# The Biggest Hits When You Were 10

Whistled by your father, hummed by your sister or overheard on the radio, these are the hit records as you reached double digits.

Don McLean 🎵 American Pie
Chicago 🎵 Saturday in the Park
3 Dog Night 🎵 Never Been to Spain
Neil Young 🎵 Heart of Gold
Harry Nilsson 🎵 Without You
Hot Butter 🎵 Popcorn
Bill Withers 🎵 Lean on Me
Jerry Lee Lewis 🎵 Chantilly Lace
Sammy Davis Jr. 🎵 The Candyman
Cat Stevens 🎵 Morning Has Broken
Looking Glass 🎵 Brandy (You're a Fine Girl)
John Fogerty
and the Blue Ridge Rangers 🎵 Jambalaya (On the Bayou)
Billy Paul 🎵 Me and Mrs. Jones
Donna Fargo 🎵 The Happiest Girl in the Whole USA
Stevie Wonder 🎵 Superstition
Elton John 🎵 Crocodile Rock
The Main Ingredient 🎵 Everybody Plays the Fool
Faron Young 🎵 It's Four in the Morning
The Moody Blues 🎵 Nights in White Satin
Harold Melvin
and the Blue Notes 🎵 If You Don't Know Me by Now
Roberta Flack 🎵 The First Time Ever I Saw Your Face
The Staple Singers 🎵 I'll Take You There
Gilbert O'Sullivan 🎵 Alone Again (Naturally)
Dr. Hook and
the Medicine Show 🎵 The Cover of the Rolling Stone

# Faster, Easier, Better

Yesterday's technological breakthrough is today's modern convenience. Here are some of the lab and engineering marvels that were made before you turned 21 years old.

| | |
|---|---|
| 1962 | Red LED |
| 1963 | **Computer mouse** |

The inventor of the computer mouse had patented it in 1963. However, by the time the mouse became commercially available in the 1980s, his patent had expired. The first computer system that made use of a (giant) mouse came from Xerox in 1981.

| | |
|---|---|
| 1964 | Plasma display |
| 1965 | Hypertext (http) |
| 1966 | Computer RAM |
| 1967 | Hand-held calculator |
| 1968 | Virtual Reality |
| 1969 | Laser printer |
| 1970 | **Wireless local area network** |

The first wireless local network was developed by the University of Hawaii to communicate data among the Hawaiian Islands.

| | |
|---|---|
| 1971 | Email |
| 1972 | Video games console (Magnavox Odyssey) |
| 1973 | Mobile phone |
| 1974 | Universal Product Code |
| 1975 | Ethernet |
| 1976 | Apple Computer |
| 1977 | Human-powered aircraft |
| 1978 | BBS (Bulletin Board System) |
| 1979 | Compact disc |
| 1980 | Pac-Man |
| 1981 | Graphic User Interface (GUI) |
| 1982 | **Emoticons** |

The inventor of the smiley emoticon hands out "Smiley" cookies every September 19th—the anniversary of the first time it was used.

# Across the Nation

Double digits at last: you're old enough to eavesdrop on adults and scan the headlines. These may be some of the earliest national news stories you remember.

- ✦ Nixon wins re-election
- ✦ The world's greatest jewel heist? Eight rob the Pierre Hotel
- ✦ Dallas Cowboys win the Super Bowl
- ✦ Shirley Chisholm announces her run for president
- ✦ Bob Douglas elected to Basketball Hall of Fame
- ✦ Equal Rights Amendment passes
- ✦ President Nixon visits China
- ✦ Coal sludge spill kills over 125
- ✦ Gov. George Wallace shot while campaigning for presidency
- ✦ Watergate burglars arrested
- ✦ Black Hills Flood strikes
- ✦ Hurricane Agnes hits the East Coast
- ✦ No new draftees to Vietnam announced
- ✦ Supreme Court rules death penalty unconstitutional
- ✦ Actress Jane Fonda tours Vietnam
- ✦ Health officials admit to Tuskegee study scandal
- ✦ Swimmer Mark Spitz wins 7 Olympic gold medals
- ✦ Riot breaks out on USS Kitty Hawk
- ✦ FBI hires first female agents
- ✦ HBO begins as subscription cable-provider service
- ✦ Apollo 17 returns safely
- ✦ Football's "Immaculate Reception" completed
- ✦ Women run the Boston Marathon
- ✦ Black Lung Benefit bill signed

*Born this year:*
- ⚭ Rapper Eminem
- ⚭ Actress Cameron Diaz
- ⚭ Actor Ben Affleck

# Kapow! Comic Books and Heroes from Your Childhood

Barely a year went past in the mid-20th Century without a new super-powered hero arriving to save the day. Here are some that were taking on the bad guys during your childhood.

*Tales of Suspense* ✳ Captain America

*Sgt. Fury & His Howling Commandos* ✳ **Nick Fury**
The title was chosen as a bet: co-creator Stan Lee reckoned that he and Jack Kirby could find success with a silly name—and they did just that.

*Strange Tales* ✳ Doctor Strange

*Showcase* ✳ The Spectre

*Iron Man* ✳ Iron Man

*The Phantom Stranger* ✳ The Phantom Stranger

*The Flash* ✳ Wally West

*Green Lantern* ✳ Hal Jordan

*Adventure Comics* ✳ Supergirl

*Fantastic Four* ✳ The Thing

*The Tomb of Dracula* ✳ Count Dracula

*Hero For Hire* ✳ Luke Cage

*Swamp Thing* ✳ Swamp Thing

*Action Comics* ✳ Superman

*Wonder Woman* ✳ Wonder Woman

*The Avengers* ✳ Thor

*The Amazing Spider-Man* ✳ Spider-Man

*Detective Comics* ✳ Batman

*The X-Men* ✳ X-Men

*Daredevil* ✳ Daredevil

*The Incredible Hulk* ✳ Wolverine

*Captain America* ✳ Captain America

*Marvel Premiere* ✳ Iron Fist

*Werewolf by Night* ✳ Moon Knight

*The Deadly Hands of Kung Fu* ✳ Jack of Hearts

*Marvel Premiere* ✳ 3-D Man

# Winners of the Stanley Cup Since You Were Born

The prestigious Stanley Cup has been changing hands since 1893, although the trophy itself has been redesigned more than once. Here are the teams to lift the champagne-filled cup since you were born.

- Detroit Red Wings (4)
- Chicago Black Hawks (3)
- **Boston Bruins (3)**
  1970: Bobby Orr scored perhaps the most famous goal in NHL history, in midair, to clinch the title.

- **New York Rangers (1)**
  After a 1940 victory, the Rangers would not win another Stanley Cup for another 54 years.

- Toronto Maple Leafs (4)
- Montreal Canadiens (12)
- Philadelphia Flyers (2)
- New York Islanders (4)
- Edmonton Oilers (5)
- **Calgary Flames (1)**
  1989 was the last time a Stanley Cup Final has been played between two teams from Canada.

- Pittsburgh Penguins (5)
- New Jersey Devils (3)
- **Colorado Avalanche (2)**
  1996: A win in their first season after moving from Quebec (where their nickname was the Nordiques).

- Dallas Stars (1)
- Tampa Bay Lightning (3)
- Carolina Hurricanes (1)
- Anaheim Ducks (1)
- Los Angeles Kings (2)
- Washington Capitals (1)
- St. Louis Blues (1)

# On the Silver Screen When You Were 11

From family favorites to the films you weren't allowed to watch, these are the films and actors that drew the praise and the crowds when you turned 11.

Westworld 📽 Yul Brynner, Richard Benjamin, James Brolin

Jesus Christ Superstar 📽 Ted Neeley, Carl Anderson, Yvonne Elliman

Jonathan Livingston Seagull 📽 James Franciscus, Juliet Mills, Hal Holbrook

The Lost Horizon 📽 Peter Finch, Liv Ullmann, Sally Kellerman

Paper Moon 📽 Ryan O'Neal, Madeline Kahn, John Hillerman

The Way We Were 📽 Barbra Streisand, Robert Redford

The Sting 📽 Paul Newman, Robert Redford, Robert Shaw

The Day of the Jackal 📽 Edward Fox, Michael Lonsdale, Terence Alexander

American Graffiti 📽 Richard Dreyfuss, Ron Howard, Paul Le Mat

High Plains Drifter 📽 Verna Bloom, Billy Curtis, Buddy Van Horn

The Day of the Dolphin 📽 George C. Scott, Trish Van Devere, Paul Sorvino

**A Touch of Class** 📽 George Segal, Glenda Jackson, Paul Sorvino
**Cary Grant and Roger Moore both turned down chances to be the lead.**

Papillon 📽 Steve McQueen, Dustin Hoffman, Victory Jory

The World's Greatest Athlete 📽 John Amos, Roscoe Lee Browne, Tim Conway

Sleeper 📽 Woody Allen, Diane Keaton, John Beck

Pat Garrett and Billy the Kid 📽 James Coburn, Kris Kristofferson, Richard Jaeckel

Robin Hood 📽 Brian Bedford, Roger Miller, Monica Evans

Serpico 📽 Al Pacino, John Randolph, Jack Kehoe

Battle for the Planet of the Apes 📽 Roddy McDowell, Claude Akins, Natalie Trundy

Live and Let Die 📽 Roger Moore, Yaphet Kotto, Jane Seymour

Magnum Force 📽 Clint Eastwood, Hal Holbrook, Mitchell Ryan

Enter the Dragon 📽 Jim Kelly, John Saxon, Ahna Capri

The Exorcist 📽 Ellen Burstyn, Max von Sydow, Linda Blair

The Last Detail 📽 Jack Nicholson, Otis Young, Randy Quaid

# Comic Strips You'll Know

Comic strips took off in the late 19th century and for much of the 20th century they were a dependable feature of everyday life. Some were solo efforts; others became so-called zombie strips, living on well beyond their creator. A century on, some are still going. But how many from your youth will you remember?

| | |
|---|---|
| 1940–52 | The Spirit by Will Eisner |
| 1930– | **Blondie** |
| | In 1995, Blondie was one of 20 strips commemorated by the US Postal Service in the Comic Strip Classics series. |
| 1931– | **Dick Tracy** |
| | Gould's first idea? A detective called Plainclothes Tracy. |
| 1930–95 | Mickey Mouse |
| 1932– | Mary Worth |
| 1936– | **The Phantom** |
| | Lee Falk worked on The Phantom for 63 years and Mandrake The Magician for 65. |
| 1919– | Barney Google and Snuffy Smith |
| 1938– | Nancy |
| 1946– | Mark Trail |
| 1937– | **Prince Valiant** |
| | Edward, the Duke of Windsor (previously Edward VIII), called Prince Valiant the "greatest contribution to English literature in the past hundred years." |
| 1934–2003 | **Flash Gordon** |
| | Alex Raymond created Flash Gordon to compete with the Buck Rogers comic strip. |
| 1934–77 | Li'l Abner by Al Capp |
| 1925–74 | Etta Kett by Paul Robinson |
| 1947–69 | Grandma by Charles Kuhn |
| 1948– | Rex Morgan, M.D. |
| 1933–87 | Brick Bradford |
| 1950–2000 | **Peanuts by Charles M. Schulz** |
| | Schultz was inducted into the Hockey Hall of Fame after building the Redwood Empire Arena near his studio. |
| 1950– | Beetle Bailey |

# Biggest Hits by The King

He may have conquered rock'n'roll, but Elvis's success straddled genres including country music, R&B, and more. These are his Number 1s from across the charts and across the years, beginning before you were born with the rockabilly "I Forgot…" through the posthumous country hit, "Guitar Man."

I Forgot to Remember to Forget (1955)

Heartbreak Hotel (1956)

I Want You, I Need You, I Love You (1956)

Don't Be Cruel (1956)

Hound Dog (1956)

Love Me Tender (1956)

Too Much (1957)

All Shook Up (1957)

(Let Me Be Your) Teddy Bear (1957)

Jailhouse Rock (1957)

Don't (1957)

Wear My Ring Around Your Neck (1958)

Hard Headed Woman (1958)

A Big Hunk O' Love (1959)

Stuck On You (1960)

It's Now or Never (1960)

Are You Lonesome Tonight? (1960)

Surrender (1961)

Good Luck Charm (1962)

Suspicious Minds (1969)

Moody Blue (1976)

Way Down (1977)

Guitar Man (1981)

# Childhood Candies

In labs across the country, mid-century food scientists dreamed up new and colorful ways to delight children just like you. These are the fruits of their labor, launched before you turned twenty-one.

| | |
|---|---|
| 1962 | Now and Later (Phoenix Candy Company) |
| 1962 | LemonHead (Ferrara Candy Company) |
| 1963 | **Cadbury Creme Eggs** (Fry's) |

An original 1963 Fry's Creme Egg (as they were then called) was discovered in 2017. It hasn't been eaten.

| | |
|---|---|
| 1964 | 100 Grand Bar (Nestle) |
| 1960s | Spree (Sunline Candy Company) |
| 1966 | Razzles (Fleer) |
| 1967 | **M&M Fruit Chewies** (Mars) |

In 1960, Mars launched "Opal Fruits" in the UK, possibly after a competition entry from a boy named Peter. Seven years later, they appeared in the US as Starburst. It took 20 years for the name to be standardized worldwide.

| | |
|---|---|
| 1968 | Caramello Bar (Cadbury) |
| 1971 | Laffy Taffy (Beich's) |
| 1972 | Bottle Caps (Nestle/Willy Wonka) |
| 1973 | **Marathon Bar** (Mars) |

Eight inches of chocolate-covered caramel, Marathon was only sold for 8 short years. You can still buy it in the UK, where it's called a Curly-Wurly…and what was once sold as a Marathon is now Snickers.

| | |
|---|---|
| 1979 | Skittles (Mars) |
| 1975 | **Pop Rocks** (General Foods) |

Contrary to internet rumor, you won't explode if you drink soda pop and eat Pop Rocks. But you might belch.

| | |
|---|---|
| 1976 | Everlasting Gobstoppers (Breaker Confections / Willy Wonka) |
| 1978 | Whatchamacallit Bar (Hershey's) |
| 1978 | Reese's Pieces (Hershey's) |
| 1979 | **Twix** (Mars) |

It took 12 years for Twix to cross the Atlantic after its 1967 UK launch.

# Books of the Decade

Ten years of your life that took you from adventure books aged 10 to dense works of profundity at 20—or perhaps just grown-up adventures! How many did you read when they were first published?

| | |
|---|---|
| 1972 | Watership Down by Richard Adams |
| 1972 | The Joy of Sex by Alex Comfort |
| 1972 | Fear and Loathing in Las Vegas by Hunter S. Thompson |
| 1973 | Fear of Flying by Erica Jong |
| 1973 | Gravity's Rainbow by Thomas Pynchon |
| 1974 | Jaws by Peter Benchley |
| 1974 | The Front Runner by Patricia Nell Warren |
| 1975 | The Eagle Has Landed by Jack Higgins |
| 1975 | Shōgun by James Clavell |
| 1975 | Ragtime by E.L. Doctorow |
| 1976 | Roots by Alex Haley |
| 1976 | The Hite Report by Shere Hite |
| 1977 | The Thorn Birds by Colleen McCullough |
| 1977 | The Women's Room by Marilyn French |
| 1978 | Eye of the Needle by Ken Follett |
| 1978 | The World According to Garp by John Irving |
| 1979 | Flowers in the Attic by V.C. Andrews |
| 1979 | The Hitchhiker's Guide to the Galaxy by Douglas Adams |
| 1979 | Sophie's Choice by William Styron |
| 1980 | Rage of Angels by Sidney Sheldon |
| 1980 | The Bourne Identity by Robert Ludlum |
| 1980 | The Covenant by James Michener |
| 1981 | The Hotel New Hampshire by John Irving |
| 1981 | Noble House by James Clavell |
| 1981 | An Indecent Obsession by Colleen McCullough |

# US Buildings

Some were loathed then, loved now; others, the reverse. Some broke new architectural ground; others housed famous or infamous businesses, or helped to power a nation. All of them were built in your first 18 years.

| | |
|---|---|
| 1962 | Kennedy Space Center, Florida |
| 1963 | **MetLife Building, New York City**<br>The largest office space in the world when it opened, the MetLife was born as the Pan Am Building, complete with heliport and 15 ft. lit signage atop (the last permitted). |
| 1964 | 277 Park Avenue, New Yor City |
| 1965 | Cheyenne Mountain complex, Colorado |
| 1966 | John F. Kennedy Federal Building, Boston |
| 1967 | Watergate Hotel and Office Complex |
| 1968 | **John Hancock Center, Chicago**<br>Second-highest in the world when it opened, the tower is still a creditable 33rd tallest when measured to the tip of its antenna. |
| 1969 | Transamerica Pyramid, San Francisco |
| 1970 | World Trade Center Twin Towers |
| 1971 | Blue Cross Blue Shield of Michigan, Detroit |
| 1972 | One Astor Plaza, New York City |
| 1973 | **Sears Tower (now Willis Tower), Chicago**<br>Sears Tower was the world's tallest building for nearly a quarter of a century. It was first climbed (on the outside) in 1981. |
| 1974 | New York Merchandise Mart |
| 1975 | **J. Edgar Hoover Building**<br>The FBI's Brutalist HQ exterior was originally intended to be clad with polished panels. Reviled by many, estimates for renovating it run to around US$1 billion. |
| 1976 | Verizon Building, New York City |
| 1977 | Citigroup Center, New York City |
| 1978 | 650 Fifth Ave, New York City |
| 1979 | Coca-Cola headquarters, Atlanta |
| 1980 | Plaza of the Americas, Dallas |

# Radio DJs from Your Childhood

If the radio was the soundtrack to your life as you grew up, some of these voices were part of the family. (The stations listed are where these DJs made their name; the dates are their radio broadcasting career).

Wolfman Jack 🎙 XERB/Armed Forces Radio (1960–1995)

Jocko Henderson 🎙 WDAS/W LIB (1952–1991)

**Casey Kasem** 🎙 KRLA (1954–2010)
Kasem was the host of American Top 40 for four decades. By 1986, his show was broadcast on 1,000 radio stations.

Bruce Morrow 🎙 WABC (1959–)

**Murray Kaufman** 🎙 WINS (1958–1975)
You'll likely remember him as Murray the K, the self-declared "fifth Beatle" (he played a lot of music from the Fab Four).

**Alison Steele** 🎙 WNEW-FM (1966–1995)
Aka The Nightbird, Steele was that rarity of the sixties and seventies: a successful female DJ.

**Alan Freed** 🎙 WJW/WINS (1945–1965)
Freed's career crashed after he was found to have been taking payola. His contribution was recognized posthumously when admitted into the Rock n Roll Hall of Fame.

Robert W. Morgan 🎙 KHJ-AM (1955–1998)

Dan Ingram 🎙 WABC (1958–2004)

**Dave Hull** 🎙 KRLA (1955–2010)
Another candidate for the "fifth Beatle," Hull interviewed the band many times.

Hal Jackson 🎙 WBLS (1940–2011)

Johnny Holliday 🎙 KYA (1956–)

**Herb Kent** 🎙 WVON (1944–2016)
"Cool Gent" Herb Kent was the longest-serving DJ on the radio.

Tom Donahue 🎙 WIBG/KYA (1949–1975)

John R. 🎙 WLAC (1941–1973)

Bill Randle 🎙 WERE/WCBS (1940s–2004)

**Jack Spector** 🎙 WMCA (1955–1994)
Spector, one of WMCA's "Good Guys," died on air in 1994. A long silence after playing "I'm in the Mood for Love" alerted station staff.

# It Happened in 1978

Here's a round-up of the most newsworthy events from across the US in the year you turned (sweet) 16.

- ✦ Copyright Act comes into effect
- ✦ Great Blizzard strikes
- ✦ Serial killer Ted Bundy arrested
- ✦ Karl Wallenda dies from falling from high wire
- ✦ Baseball's Pete Rose makes his 3000th hit
- ✦ Atlantic City opens for gambling
- ✦ Health crisis discovered in Love Canal
- ✦ Santa Barbara hit by earthquake
- ✦ Camp David Accords begin
- ✦ Law signed that enables minting the Susan B. Anthony dollar
- ✦ Homebrewing beer becomes legal
- ✦ Mass suicide and murder at Jonestown (right)
- ✦ Women selected as astronauts
- ✦ Double Eagle II completes its flight across the Atlantic
- ✦ Garfield the cat appears in comics
- ✦ Teachers strike across the country
- ✦ Space Invaders devours quarters
- ✦ Cellular mobile phone system created
- ✦ Dallas Cowboys win the Super Bowl
- ✦ New York Yankees win the World Series
- ✦ Making a right turn at a red light is legal nationwide
- ✦ Home Depot founded
- ✦ All-chocolate version of Monopoly released for $600
- ✦ Twinkie defense used in a murder trial

*Born this year:*
- ✾ Basketball player Kobe Bryant
- ✾ Singer John Legend
- ✾ Singer Nicole Scherzinger

FBI agents comb through the records and belongings left by Peoples Temple after the mass suicide in Jonestown, Guyana, in November 1978. Hundreds of followers of Jim Jones committed suicide—not all of them willingly—and a third of the 909 dead were children. Suicide drills had been held in anticipation of a showdown. After concerns were raised by relatives, an investigative mission headed to the commune, led by Congressman Leo Ryan. The visit turned sour and Ryan was attacked; Ryan and four others were killed at the airstrip as they tried to leave. Later that day, Jones gave his deadly orders.

# News Anchors of the Fifties and Sixties

Trusted, familiar, and exclusively male: these are the faces that brought your family the news as you took your first steps, and the catchphrases they made their own.

**Edward R. Murrow** 📺 CBS (1938-59)
"Good night, and good luck."

**Walter Cronkite** 📺 CBS (1962-81)
"And that's the way it is."

**David Brinkley** 📺 NBC (1956-71)
"Good night, Chet…"

**Chet Huntley** 📺 NBC (1956-70)
"…Good night, David."

Harry Reasoner 📺 CBS & ABC (1961-91)

Frank Reynolds 📺 ABC (1968-70)

**John Charles Daly** 📺 CBS & ABC (1941-60)
"Good night and a good tomorrow."

Douglas Edwards 📺 CBS (1948-62)

Hugh Downs 📺 NBC (1962-71)

John Chancellor 📺 NBC (1970-82)

**Paul Harvey** 📺 ABC Radio (1951-2009)
"Hello Americans, this is Paul Harvey. Stand by for news!"

Mike Wallace 📺 CBS (1963-66)

**John Cameron Swayze** 📺 NBC (1948-56)
"Well, that's the story, folks! This is John Cameron Swayze, and I'm glad we could get together."

Ron Cochran 📺 ABC (1962-65)

Bob Young 📺 ABC (1967-68)

Dave Garroway 📺 NBC (1952-61)

Bill Shadel 📺 ABC (1960-63)

# Early TV Game Shows

It all started so well: appointment radio became appointment TV, with new and crossover game shows bringing us together. But as the decade progressed, the scandal emerged: some shows were fixed. Quiz shows were down, but certainly not out. (Dates include periods off-air.)

Break the Bank 🎙 (1945-57)

Beat The Clock 🎙 (1950-2019)

**Name That Tune** 🎙 (1952-85)
A radio crossover that spawned 25 international versions.

Strike It Rich 🎙 (1947-58)

**The Price Is Right** 🎙 (1956-65)
The original version of the current quiz that began in 1972. This one was hosted by Bill Cullen.

Down You Go 🎙 (1951-56)

I've Got A Secret 🎙 (1952-2006)

What's The Story 🎙 (1951-55)

The $64,000 Question 🎙 (1955-58)

People Are Funny 🎙 (1942-60)

**Tic-Tac-Dough** 🎙 (1956-90)
Early Tic-Tac-Dough contestants were often coached; around three-quarters of the shows in one run were rigged.

The Name's The Same 🎙 (1951-55)

Two For The Money 🎙 (1952-57)

The Big Payoff 🎙 (1951-62)

**Twenty-One** 🎙 (1956-58)
At the heart of the rigging scandal, Twenty-One was the subject of Robert Redford's 1994 movie, Quiz Show.

Masquerade Party 🎙 (1952-60)

**You Bet Your Life** 🎙 (1947-61)
A comedy quiz hosted by Groucho Marx.

**Truth or Consequences** 🎙 (1940-88)
Started life as a radio quiz. TV host Bob Barker signed off with: "Hoping all your consequences are happy ones."

20 Questions 🎙 (1946-55)

What's My Line 🎙 (1950-75)

# Liberty Issue Stamps

First released in 1954, the Liberty Issue drew its name from not one but three depictions of the Statue of Liberty across the denominations. (There was only room for one "real" woman, though.) It coincided with the new era of stamp collecting as a childhood hobby that endured for decades. Were you one of these new miniature philatelists?

**Benjamin Franklin** ½ ¢ 🖃 Polymath (writer, inventor, scientist)
Franklin discovered the principle of electricity,
the Law of Conservation of Charge.

George Washington 1 ¢ 🖃 First US President
**Palace of the Governors** 1 ¼ ¢ 🖃
A building in Santa Fe, New Mexico that served as
the seat of government of New Mexico for centuries.

Mount Vernon 1 ½ ¢ 🖃 George Washington's plantation
Thomas Jefferson 2 ¢ 🖃 Polymath; third US President
Bunker Hill Monument 2 ½ ¢ 🖃 Battle site of the Revolutionary War
Statue of Liberty 3 ¢ 🖃 Gifted by the people of France
**Abraham Lincoln** 4 ¢ 🖃 16th US President
Lincoln received a patent for a flotation device that assisted
boats in moving through shallow water.

The Hermitage 4 ½ ¢ 🖃 Andrew Jackson's plantation
James Monroe 5 ¢ 🖃 Fifth US President
Theodore Roosevelt 6 ¢ 🖃 26th US President
Woodrow Wilson 7 ¢ 🖃 28th US President; served during WW1
John J. Pershing 8 ¢ 🖃 US Army officer during World War I
Alamo 9 ¢ 🖃 Site of a pivotal Texas Revolution battle
Independence Hall 10 ¢ 🖃 Independence declared here
Benjamin Harrison 12 ¢ 🖃 23rd US President
John Jay 15 ¢ 🖃 First Chief Justice of the United States
Monticello 20 ¢ 🖃 Thomas Jefferson's plantation
Paul Revere 25 ¢ 🖃 Alerted militia of the British approach
Robert E. Lee 30 ¢ 🖃 Confederate general in the Civil War
John Marshall 40 ¢ 🖃 Fourth Chief Justice of the US
Susan B. Anthony 50 ¢ 🖃 Women's suffrage activist
Patrick Henry $1 🖃 Leader of the Dec. of Independence
Alexander Hamilton $5 🖃 First Secretary of the Treasury

# The Biggest Hits
# When You Were 16

The artists that topped the charts when you turned 16 might not be in your top 10 these days, but you'll probably remember them!

Kenny Rogers 🎵 The Gambler

Waylon Jennings
and Willie Nelson 🎵 Mamas Don't Let Your Babies
Grow Up to Be Cowboys

The Bee Gees 🎵 Night Fever

Frankie Valli 🎵 Grease

Village People 🎵 Y.M.C.A.

John Travolta
and Olivia Newton-John 🎵 You're the One That I Want

Exile 🎵 Kiss You All Over

Player 🎵 Baby Come Back

Crystal Gayle 🎵 Talking in Your Sleep

Chic 🎵 Le Freak

Rod Stewart 🎵 Do Ya Think I'm Sexy?

Quincy Jones 🎵 Stuff Like That

The Rolling Stones 🎵 Miss You

Olivia Newton-John 🎵 A Little More Love

A Taste of Honey 🎵 Boogie Oogie Oogie

Roberta Flack
and Donny Hathaway 🎵 The Closer I Get to You

Anne Murray 🎵 You Needed Me

Andy Gibb 🎵 Shadow Dancing

Paul McCartney and Wings 🎵 With a Little Luck

Foreigner 🎵 Hot Blooded

Chaka Khan 🎵 I'm Every Woman

Steve Martin 🎵 King Tut

The Commodores 🎵 Three Times a Lady

Kansas 🎵 Dust in the Wind

# Medical Advances Before You Were 21

A baby born in 1920 USA had a life expectancy of just 55.4 years. By 2000 that was up to 76.8, thanks to medical advances including many of these.

| | |
|---|---|
| 1962 | Hip replacement |
| 1962 | Beta blocker |
| 1962 | First oral polio vaccine (Sabin) |
| 1963 | Liver and lung transplants |
| 1963 | Valium |
| 1963 | Artificial heart |
| 1964 | Measles vaccine |
| 1965 | Portable defibrillator |
| 1965 | Commercial ultrasound |
| 1966 | Pancreas transplant |
| 1967 | Mumps vaccine |
| 1967 | Heart transplant |
| 1968 | Powered prosthesis |
| 1968 | Controlled drug delivery |
| 1969 | Balloon catheter |
| 1969 | Cochlear implant |
| 1971 | CAT scan |
| 1972 | Insulin pump |
| 1973 | MRI Scanning |
| 1973 | Laser eye surgery (LASIK) |
| 1974 | **Liposuction**<br>Liposuction did not become popular until 1985 when techniques had improved to decrease the patient developing serious bleeding. |
| 1976 | First commercial PET scanner |
| 1977 | Pneumonia vaccine |
| 1978 | "Test-tube" baby (IVF) |
| 1979 | Last case of smallpox reported |
| 1980 | MRI whole body scanner |
| 1981 | Artificial skin |
| 1981 | Heart-lung transplant |

# Blockbuster Movies When You Were 16

These are the movies that everyone was talking about. How many of them did you see (or have you seen since)?

Jaws II 📽 Roy Scheider, Lorraine Gary, Murray Hamilton

The Deer Hunter 📽 Robert De Niro, John Cazale, Meryl Streep

Revenge of the Pink Panther 📽 Peter Sellers, Herbert Lom, Robert Webber

**Superman** 📽 Marlon Brando, Gene Hackman, Christopher Reeve

**Costing $55 million, Superman was the most expensive film ever made at the time.**

Every Which Way but Loose 📽 Clint Eastwood, Sondra Locke, Geoffrey Lewis

Invasion of the Body Snatchers 📽 Donald Sutherland, Brooke Adams

Grease 📽 John Travolta, Olivia Newton-John, Stockard Channing

The Lord of the Rings 📽 Christopher Guard, William Squire, John Hurt

An Unmarried Woman 📽 Jill Clayburgh, Alan Bates, Michael Murphy

Halloween 📽 Donald Pleasence, Jamie Lee Curtis, P.J. Soles

House Calls 📽 Walter Matthau, Glenda Jackson, Art Carney

National Lampoon's Animal House 📽 John Belushi, Peter Riegert, Tim Matheson

Convoy 📽 Kris Kristofferson, Ali MacGraw, Ernest Borgnine

Foul Play 📽 Goldie Hawn, Chevy Chase, Dudley Moore

Midnight Express 📽 Brad Davis, Irene Miracle, Bo Hopkins

California Suite 📽 Jane Fonda, Alan Alda, Maggie Smith

Heaven Can Wait 📽 Warren Beatty, Julie Christie, James Mason

**The Wiz** 📽 Diana Ross, Michael Jackson, Nipsey Russell

**Diana Ross was considered too old to play Dorothy, but convinced Universal Pictures and Motown Records to relent.**

F.I.S.T. 📽 Sylvester Stallone, Rod Steiger, Peter Boyle

The End 📽 Burt Reynolds, Sally Field, Dom DeLuise

Coming Home 📽 Jane Fonda, Jon Voight, Bruce Dern

# Game Show Hosts of the Fifties and Sixties

Many of these men were semi-permanent fixtures, their voices and catchphrases ringing through the decades. Some were full-time entertainers; others were on sabbatical from more serious news duties.

John Charles Daly ▶◀ What's My Line (1950-67)

Art Linkletter ▶◀ People Are Funny (1943-60)

Garry Moore ▶◀ I've Got A Secret (1956-64)

Groucho Marx ▶◀ You Bet Your Life (1949-61)

Warren Hull ▶◀ Strike It Rich (1947-58)

Herb Shriner ▶◀ Two For The Money (1952-56)

George DeWitt ▶◀ Name That Tune (1953-59)

Robert Q. Lewis ▶◀ Name's The Same (1951-54)

Bill Cullen ▶◀ The Price Is Right (1956-65)

**Walter Cronkite** ▶◀ It's News To Me (1954)
"The most trusted man in America" was briefly the host of this topical quiz game. He didn't do it again.

Bill Slater ▶◀ 20 Questions (1949-52)

Walter Kiernan ▶◀ Who Said That (1951-54)

Bob Eubanks ▶◀ The Newlywed Game (1966-74)

Bud Collyer ▶◀ To Tell The Truth (1956-69)

Jack Barry ▶◀ Twenty-One (1956-58)

Bert Parks ▶◀ Break The Bank (1945-57)

Hugh Downs ▶◀ Concentration (1958-69)

Mike Stokey ▶◀ Pantomime Quiz (1947-59)

Allen Ludden ▶◀ Password (1961-75)

**Bob Barker** ▶◀ Truth or Consequences (1956-74)
Barker also spent 35 years hosting The Price Is Right.

Hal March ▶◀ $64,000 Question (1955-58)

**Monty Hall** ▶◀ Let's Make A Deal (1963-91)
Monty—born "Monte", but misspelled on an early publicity photo—was also a philanthropist who raised around $1 billion over his lifetime.

Johnny Carson ▶◀ Who Do You Trust? (1957-63)

# Kitchen Inventions

The 20th-century kitchen was a playground for food scientists and engineers with new labor-saving devices and culinary shortcuts launched every year. These all made their debut before you were 18.

| | |
|---|---|
| 1962 | Chimney starter |
| 1963 | **Veg-O-Matic**<br>The Veg-O-Matic has increased the cultural lexicon in a number of ways, including "As Seen On TV" and "It slices and dices." |
| 1964 | Pop Tarts |
| 1965 | Bounty paper towels |
| 1966 | Cool Whip |
| 1967 | Countertop microwave |
| 1968 | Hunt snack pack |
| 1969 | Manwich |
| 1970 | Hamburger Helper |
| 1971 | **Crock Pot**<br>The hit show "This is Us" featured a tragic house fire caused directly by a defective Crock Pot. The company released an ad campaign to diffuse the publicity. |
| 1972 | Mr. Coffee |
| 1973 | Dawn dishwashing soap |
| 1974 | Fajita |
| 1975 | Famous Amos cookies |
| 1976 | Ginsu knives |
| 1977 | Slim Fast |
| 1978 | Microwavable popcorn bag |
| 1979 | Black & Decker Dustbuster |

# Around the World When You Turned 18

These are the headlines from around the globe as you were catapulted into adulthood.

+ Rubik's Cube debuts at London toy fair
+ Iraq invades Iran
+ Mini gold rush occurs in Australia
+ Mugabe is elected
+ Israel replaces the pound with the shekel
+ Terrorists bomb Italian railway, killing 70
+ Hurricane Allen makes landfall in Jamaica and Haiti
+ Oil platform collapses in North Sea
+ Zimbabwe becomes majority Black-ruled
+ Polish shipyard workers begin strike
+ Japan becomes the world's leading auto maker
+ Moscow Olympic Games
+ President Tito dies
+ Indira Gandhi becomes PM again
+ Julianna of the Netherlands abdicates as queen
+ Thousands flee Cuba by boat
+ Rock festival is held in Soviet Union
+ Plane bound for Tenerife crashes, killing 146
+ Iceland elects woman as president
+ Powerful earthquake kills thousands in Algeria
+ Greece rejoins NATO
+ Protestors in South Korea shot by army
+ Spanish embassy set on fire in Guatemala
+ Embassy in Colombia is attacked by terrorists
+ Italy hit by earthquake

# Super Bowl Champions Since You Were Born

These are the teams that have held a 7-pound, sterling silver Vince Lombardi trophy aloft during the Super Bowl era, and the number of times they've done it in your lifetime.

- **New England Patriots (6)**
  2001: The Super Bowl MVP, Tom Brady, had been a 6th round draft pick in 2000.

- Pittsburgh Steelers (6)
- Dallas Cowboys (5)
- San Francisco 49ers (5)
- **Green Bay Packers (4)**
  1967: To gain a berth in the Super Bowl, the Packers defeated the Dallas Cowboys in The Ice Bowl at 15 degrees below zero.

- New York Giants (4)
- **Denver Broncos (3)**
  2015: After the Broncos won their first Super Bowl 18 years prior, Broncos owner Pat Bowlen dedicated the victory to long-time quarterback John Elway ("This one's for John!"). After the 2015 victory, John Elway (now general manager) dedicated it to the ailing Bowlen ("This one's for Pat!").

- Washington Football Team (3)
- Las Vegas Raiders (3)
- Miami Dolphins (2)
- Indianapolis Colts (2)
- Kansas City Chiefs (2)
- Baltimore Ravens (2)
- Tampa Bay Buccaneers (2)
- **St. Louis/Los Angeles Rams (2)**
  1999: The Rams were led to the Super Bowl by Kurt Warner, who had been a grocery store clerk after college.

- Seattle Seahawks (1)
- Philadelphia Eagles (1)
- **Chicago Bears (1)**
  The 1985 Bears are known for their song, The Super Bowl Shuffle.

- New York Jets (1)
- New Orleans Saints (1)

# Across the Nation

**18**

Voting. Joining the military. Turning 18 is serious stuff. Here's what everyone was reading about in the year you reached this milestone.

- Mount St. Helens erupts
- CNN begins broadcasting
- Staggers Act deregulates the rail industry (1st time since 1887)
- Post-it Notes go on sale
- Men's hockey team beats Soviets on way to Olympic gold
- John Lennon shot
- Fire at MGM Grand Hotel kills 85
- Rioting in Miami leaves 17 dead
- Lake Placid hosts Winter Olympics
- Ronald Reagan elected president
- Operation to rescue hostages in Iran fails
- Boycott of Summer Olympics over Soviet invasion of Afghanistan
- Cubans flee Cuba in the Mariel Boatlift
- Far Side cartoon begins publication
- Big League Chew gum goes on sale
- All men (18-25 years old) have to sign up for selective service
- Severe heat wave strikes
- Philadelphia Phillies win the World Series
- Super Bowl winners are again the Pittsburgh Steelers
- Jack Nicklaus takes the US Open
- John McEnroe and Chris Evert rule the tennis courts
- Rubik's Cube begins to puzzle people
- Killer Clown John Wayne Gacy sentenced to death
- Arthur Ashe retires from tennis

*Born this year:*
- Actor Macaulay Culkin
- TV star Kim Kardashian
- Actress Christina Ricci
- Singer Christina Aguilera

Three days after John Lennon was shot and killed on December 8, 1980, the shock is still written on the face of fans. They're gathered outside the Dakota Building where Mark Chapman calmly waited to be arrested, holding a copy of The Catcher in the Rye. There was no funeral; in its place, Yoko requested ten minutes' silence. And on the following Sunday, every New York radio station heeded her call.

# US Open Champions

Winners while you were between the ages of the youngest (John McDermott, 1911, 19 years) and the oldest (Hale Irwin, 1990, at 45). Planning a win? Better hurry up!

| | |
|---|---|
| 1981 | David Graham |
| 1982 | Tom Watson |
| 1983 | Larry Nelson |
| 1984 | Fuzzy Zoeller |
| 1985 | Andy North |
| 1986 | Raymond Floyd |
| 1987 | Scott Simpson |
| 1988 | Curtis Strange |
| 1989 | Curtis Strange |

Strange's successful defense of his US Open title wouldn't be repeated for nearly 30 years (by Brooks Koepka, in 2018).

| | |
|---|---|
| 1990 | Hale Irwin |
| 1991 | Payne Stewart |
| 1992 | Tom Kite |
| 1993 | Lee Janzen |
| 1994 | Ernie Els |
| 1995 | Corey Pavin |
| 1996 | Steve Jones |
| 1997 | Ernie Els |
| 1998 | Lee Janzen |
| 1999 | Payne Stewart |
| 2000 | **Tiger Woods** |

Woods won by 15 strokes, the largest margin ever.

| | |
|---|---|
| 2001 | Retief Goosen |
| 2002 | Tiger Woods |
| 2003 | Jim Furyk |
| 2004 | Retief Goosen |
| 2005 | Michael Campbell |
| 2006 | Geoff Ogilvy |
| 2007 | Angel Cabrera |

# Popular Girls' Names

If you started a family at a young age, these are the names you're most likely to have chosen. And even if you didn't pick them, a lot of Americans did!

Jennifer
Jessica
Amanda
Sarah
Melissa
Nicole
Stephanie
**Elizabeth**
A name's moment in the sun spans years, sometimes decades. But eventually they disappear out of sight... unless you're Elizabeth. For over a century she's floated between 6th and 26th position.

Crystal
Amy
Michelle
Heather
Tiffany
Kimberly
Rebecca
Angela
Ashley
Amber
Christina
Erin
Rachel
Laura
Lisa
Emily
Kelly
**Rising and falling stars:**
Girls we welcomed for the first time this year: Cassandra, Krystal, Alexis, Brittany, Jillian and Nichole. Names we'd never see in the Top 100 again: Dawn, Lori and Denise.

# Animals Extinct in Your Lifetime

Billions of passenger pigeons once flew the US skies.
By 1914, they had been trapped to extinction. Not every
species dies at our hands, but it's a sobering roll-call.
(Date is year last known alive or declared extinct).

| | |
|---|---|
| 1962 | Red-bellied opossum, Argentina |
| 1963 | Kākāwahie honeycreeper, Hawaii |
| 1964 | South Island snipe, New Zealand |
| 1966 | Arabian ostrich |
| 1967 | Saint Helena earwig |
| 1967 | **Yellow blossom pearly mussel**<br>Habitat loss and pollution proved terminal for this Tennessee resident. |
| 1968 | Mariana fruit bat (Guam) |
| 1971 | Lake Pedder earthworm, Tasmania |
| 1972 | Bushwren, New Zealand |
| 1977 | Siamese flat-barbelled catfish, Thailand |
| 1979 | Yunnan Lake newt, China |
| 1981 | Southern gastric-brooding frog, Australia |
| 1986 | Las Vegas dace |
| 1989 | Golden toad (see right) |
| 1990 | Dusky seaside sparrow, East Coast USA |
| 1990 | Atitlán grebe, Guatemala |
| 1990s | Rotund rocksnail, USA |
| 2000 | **Pyrenean ibex, Iberia**<br>For a few minutes in 2003 this species was brought back to life through cloning, but sadly the newborn female ibex died. |
| 2001 | Caspian tiger, Central Asia |
| 2008 | Saudi gazelle |
| 2012 | **Pinta giant tortoise**<br>The rarest creature in the world for the latter half of his 100-year life, Lonesome George of the Galapagos was the last remaining Pinta tortoise. |
| 2016 | Bramble Cay melomys (a Great Barrier Reef rodent) |

The observed history of the golden toad is brief and tragic. It wasn't discovered until two years after you were born, abundant in a pristine area of Costa Rica. By 1989 it had gone, a victim of rising temperatures.

# Popular Boys' Names

Here are the top boys' names for this year. Many of the most popular choices haven't shifted much since you were born, but more modern names are creeping in…

Michael

Christopher

**Matthew**

For fourteen years from 1980, tastes in baby names were locked tight at the top: Michael was the most popular, Christopher was runner-up with Matthew in third spot.

Jason

David

James

Joshua

John

Robert

Daniel

Joseph

Justin

Ryan

Brian

William

Jonathan

Andrew

Brandon

Adam

Eric

Nicholas

Anthony

Thomas

Kevin

Timothy

Steven

**Rising and falling stars:**

Debutants in 1982: Ian, Jordan and Cody. Off into the sunset go Shaun, Russell and Jerry.

# Popular Movies When You Were 21

The biggest stars in the biggest movies: these are the films the nation were enjoying as you entered into adulthood.

High Road to China 🎬 Tom Selleck, Jack Weston, Bess Armstrong

Mr. Mom 🎬 Michael Keaton, Teri Garr, Jeffrey Tambor

Scarface 🎬 Steven Bauer, Michelle Pfeiffer

**Flashdance** 🎬 Jennifer Beals, Michael Nouri, Lilia Skala
**Maureen Marder, the original subject of Flashdance, signed away her life story rights for $2,300. The movie grossed over $200 million.**

Staying Alive 🎬 John Travolta, Cynthia Rhodes, Finola Hughes

**Terms of Endearment** 🎬 Debra Winger, Shirley MacLaine, Jack Nicholson
**Director James L. Brooks wrote the Garrett Breedlove role for Burt Reynolds, who turned it down.**

Psycho II 🎬 Anthony Perkins, Vera Miles, Robert Loggia

Risky Business 🎬 Tom Cruise, Rebecca De Mornay, Joe Pantoliano

Spacehunter 🎬 Peter Strauss, Molly Ringwald, Ernie Hudson

Superman III 🎬 Christopher Reeve, Richard Pryor, Jackie Cooper

The Outsiders 🎬 C. Thomas Howell, Rob Lowe, Emilio Estevez

Easy Money 🎬 Rodney Dangerfield, Joe Pesci, Geraldine Fitzgerald

Blue Thunder 🎬 Roy Scheider, Warren Oates, Candy Clark

Trading Places 🎬 Dan Aykroyd, Eddie Murphy, Ralph Bellamy

Never Say Never Again 🎬 Sean Connery, Klaus Maria Brandauer, Max von Sydow

Octopussy 🎬 Roger Moore, Maud Adams, Louis Jourdan

WarGames 🎬 Matthew Broderick, Ally Sheedy, John Wood

Star Wars Epi. VI: Return of the Jedi 🎬 Mark Hamill, Harrison Ford, Carrie Fisher

Yentl 🎬 Barbra Streisand, Amy Irving, Mandy Patinkin

Sudden Impact 🎬 Clint Eastwood, Sondra Locke, Pat Hingle

National Lampoon's Vacation 🎬 Chevy Chase, Beverly D'Angelo, Imogene Coca

The Big Chill 🎬 Tom Berenger, Glenn Close, Jeff Goldblum

# Across the Nation

A selection of national headlines from the year you turned 21. But how many can you remember?

- ✦ Texas coast hit by Hurricane Alicia
- ✦ Invasion of Grenada is launched (right)
- ✦ Sally Ride becomes the first woman to walk in space
- ✦ Strategic Defense Initiative (SDI) proposed
- ✦ Best Buy and Papa John's got their starts
- ✦ Earthquake hits New York
- ✦ Land speed record of 633.468 mph set in Nevada
- ✦ Truck bomb hits Marine barracks in Beirut
- ✦ Motorola releases mobile phone
- ✦ Cabbage Patch dolls go on sale
- ✦ ARPANET changes to use Internet protocols, creating the Internet
- ✦ Microsoft Word released
- ✦ IBM PC XT released
- ✦ Barney Frank dies 112 days after his artificial heart implanted
- ✦ Robbery of a gambling club in Seattle leaves 13 dead
- ✦ Vanessa Williams crowned Miss America
- ✦ Martin Luther King Day signed into law
- ✦ McNuggets are on the menu
- ✦ Washington Redskins win the Super Bowl
- ✦ Baltimore Orioles win the World Series
- ✦ Space Shuttle Challenger makes maiden flight
- ✦ Compact discs become available
- ✦ Apple IIe goes on sale
- ✦ Consumer camcorders released to the public

*Born this year:*
- ⚭ Actor Donald Glover
- ⚭ NSA whistleblower Edward Snowden
- ⚭ Actor Aziz Ansari

The invasion of the small Caribbean island nation of Grenada began at dawn on October 25, 1983. Codenamed Operation Urgent Fury, the order to restore stability and safeguard around 600 US students and holidaymakers, took US Army planners by surprise. Many had been expecting a mission to the Middle East, where 241 US marines had recently lost their lives in a truck bomb attack. Instead they improvised with tourist maps, and the island assault quickly overthrew the unstable military government and installed an interim administration. Although criticized internationally, the action was deemed "a complete success" by the commander in charge, Admiral McDonald (above).

# The Biggest Hits
# When You Were 21

The artists you love at 21 are with you for life.
How many of these hits from this milestone
year can you still hum or sing in the tub?

Duran Duran ✐ Hungry Like the Wolf
Marvin Gaye ✐ Sexual Healing
The Police ✐ Every Breath You Take
Michael Jackson ✐ Billie Jean
Prince ✐ 1999
Kenny Rogers
and Dolly Parton ✐ Islands in the Stream
Bryan Adams ✐ This Time
New Edition ✐ Candy Girl
Yes ✐ Owner of a Lonely Heart
Stevie Ray Vaughan ✐ Pride and Joy
B.J. Thomas ✐ What Ever Happened To
Old Fashioned Love
Michael Jackson ✐ Beat It
The S.O.S. Band ✐ Just Be Good To Me
Madonna ✐ Holiday
John Anderson ✐ Swingin'
Culture Club ✐ Karma Chameleon
Kenny Rogers
and Sheena Easton ✐ We've Got Tonight
Rufus and Chaka Khan ✐ Ain't Nobody
David Bowie ✐ Let's Dance
Def Leppard ✐ Rock of Ages
Irene Cara ✐ Flashdance... What a Feeling
Michael Jackson
and Paul McCartney ✐ Say Say Say
Men Without Hats ✐ Safety Dance
Mtume ✐ Juicy Fruit

# Popular Food in the 1960s

Changes in society didn't stop at the front door: a revolution in the kitchen brought us exotic new recipes, convenience in a can, and even space-age fruit flavors. These are the tastes of a decade, but how many of them were on the menu for your family?

**McDonald's Big Mac**
First served in 1967 by a Pittsburgh franchisee.
Royal Shake-a-Pudd'n Dessert Mix
Tunnel of Fudge Cake
Campbell's SpaghettiOs
Pop-Tarts
B&M's canned bread
**Cool Whip**
A time-saving delight that originally contained no milk or cream, meaning that it could be frozen and transported easily.

Grasshopper pie
Beech-Nut Fruit Stripe Gum
Sandwich Loaf
**Lipton Onion Soup Dip**
Millions of packets are still sold each year of this favorite that was once known as "Californian Dip".

Jello salad
Hires Root Beer
Baked Alaska
**Tang**
Invented by William A. Mitchell who also concocted Cool Whip, Tang was used by astronauts to flavor the otherwise unpalatable water on board the Gemini and Apollo missions.

Corn Diggers
Teem soda
Eggo Waffles
Kraft Shake 'N Bake
**Maypo oatmeal**
In 1985, Dire Straights sang, "I want my MTV"—an echo of the stars who'd shouted the same words to promote the new station. But 30 years before that (and the inspiration for MTV's campaign), an animated child yelled, "I want my Maypo!"

# Fashion in the Sixties

As a child, you (generally) wear what you're given. It's only in hindsight, on fading Polaroids, that you recognize that your outfits carried the fashion imprint of the day. Whether you were old or bold enough to carry off a pair of bell bottoms, though, is a secret that should remain between you and your photo albums.

### Bell bottoms
Bell bottoms were widely available at Navy surplus and thrift stores at a time when second-hand shopping was on the rise.

Miniskirts and mini dresses

Peasant blouses

### Rudi Gernreich
Pope Paul IV banned Catholics from wearing his monokini—a topless swim suit.

US flag clothing

Tulle turbans

Shift dresses

### Collarless jackets
This jacket trend was popularized by the Beatles in 1963.

Babydoll dresses

V-neck tennis sweaters

Afghan coats

### Leopard print clothing
In 1962, Jackie Kennedy wore a leopard print coat which caused a spike in demand for leopard skin, leading to the death of up to 250,000 leopards. The coat's designer, Oleg Cassini, felt guilty about it for the rest of his life.

Tie-dye clothing

Short, brightly colored, shapeless dresses

Pillbox hats

Mary Quant

Maxi skirts

Bonnie Cashin

Plaid

Poor boy sweaters

Pea coats

# Around the World When You Turned 25

With the growing reach of news organizations, events from outside our borders were sometimes front-page news. How many do you remember?

+ Fiji becomes a republic
+ West German pilot lands Cessna in Red Square
+ Ferry capsizes off coast of Belgium
+ Supernova that can be seen without telescopes appears
+ Hurricane-force wind strikes English coast
+ Single European Act comes in effect
+ Diesel train sets speed record in UK
+ France announces plans to build Disneyland Paris
+ Terrorists kidnap Terry Waite
+ UK elects Thatcher for third time
+ Series of bomb attacks kill over 100 in Sri Lanka
+ Hungerford shooting rampage occurs in UK
+ Fire in the Underground kills 31 in London
+ Nazi Klaus Barbie found guilty of crimes against humanity
+ Bus passengers murdered by terrorists in India
+ Supertyphoon Nina devastates the Philippines
+ Horrific ferry accident in Manila kills 4,000
+ President of Ecuador is kidnapped, later released
+ Rugby World Cup begins in New Zealand
+ Martial Law ends in Taiwan after almost 40 years
+ F4 tornado strikes Edmonton, Alberta
+ Rudolf Hess dies in prison
+ Elizabeth II opens Order of the Garter to include women
+ Iranian pilgrims clash with authorities at Mecca
+ New Zealand becomes a Nuclear-Free Zone

# Cars of the 1960s

Smaller cars. More powerful cars. More distinctive cars. More variety, yes: but the success of imported models such as the Volkswagen Beetle was a sign that more fundamental changes lay ahead for The Big Three.

| | |
|---|---|
| 1940 | Ford Lincoln Continental |
| 1949 | Volkswagen Beetle |
| 1950 | Volkswagen Type 2 (Microbus) |
| 1958 | **General Motors Chevrolet Impala**<br>In 1965, the Impala sold more than 1 million units, the most sold by any model in the US since WWII. |
| 1958 | American Motors Corporation Rambler Ambassador |
| 1959 | General Motors Chevrolet El Camino |
| 1959 | Ford Galaxie |
| 1960 | **Ford Falcon**<br>The cartoon strip "Peanuts" was animated for TV to market the Falcon. |
| 1960 | General Motors Pontiac Tempest |
| 1960 | General Motors Chevrolet Corvair |
| 1961 | **Jaguar E-Type**<br>Ranked first in The Daily Telegraph UK's list of the world's "100 most beautiful cars" of all time. |
| 1961 | Chrysler Newport |
| 1962 | Shelby Cobra |
| 1963 | General Motors Buick Riviera |
| 1963 | Porsche 911 |
| 1963 | Kaiser-Jeep Jeep Wagoneer |
| 1964 | **Ford Mustang**<br>The song of the same name reached #6 on the R&B Charts in 1966. That year, more Ford Mustangs were sold (550,000) than any other car. |
| 1964 | General Motors Chevrolet Chevelle |
| 1964 | Chrysler Plymouth Barracuda |
| 1964 | General Motors Pontiac GTO |
| 1967 | General Motors Chevrolet Camaro |
| 1967 | Ford Mercury Cougar |
| 1968 | Chrysler Plymouth Road Runner |

# Books of the Decade

Were you a voracious bookworm in your twenties? Or a more reluctant reader, only drawn by the biggest titles of the day? Here are the new titles that fought for your attention.

|  |  |
|------|-------|
| 1982 | The Color Purple by Alice Walker |
| 1982 | Space by James A. Michener |
| 1983 | Pet Sematary by Stephen King |
| 1983 | Hollywood Wives by Jackie Collins |
| 1984 | You Can Heal Your Life by Louise Hay |
| 1984 | Money: A Suicide Note by Martin Amis |
| 1985 | The Handmaid's Tale by Margaret Atwood |
| 1985 | White Noise by Don DeLillo |
| 1985 | Lake Wobegon Days by Garrison Keillor |
| 1986 | It by Stephen King |
| 1986 | Wanderlust by Danielle Steele |
| 1987 | Patriot Games by Tom Clancy |
| 1987 | Beloved by Toni Morrison |
| 1987 | The Bonfire of the Vanities by Tom Wolfe |
| 1988 | The Cardinal of the Kremlin by Tom Clancy |
| 1988 | The Sands of Time by Sidney Sheldon |
| 1989 | Clear and Present Danger by Stephen R. Covey |
| 1989 | The Pillars of the Earth by Ken Follett |
| 1990 | The Plains of Passage by Jean M. Auel |
| 1990 | Possession by A.S. Byatt |
| 1990 | Four Past Midnight by Stephen King |
| 1991 | The Firm by John Grisham |
| 1991 | The Kitchen God's Wife by Amy Tan |
| 1991 | Scarlett by Alexandra Ripley |

# Prominent Americans

This new set of definitive stamps, issued from 1965 onwards, aimed to do a better job of capturing the diversity of the Americans who made a nation. The series doubled the previous number of women depicted...to two. How many did you have in your collection?

Thomas Jefferson 1 ¢ Third US President
Albert Gallatin 1 ¼ ¢ Fourth Treasury Secretary
Frank Lloyd Wright 2 ¢ Architect
Francis Parkman 3 ¢ Historian
Abraham Lincoln 4 ¢ 16th US President
George Washington 5 ¢ First US President
Franklin D Roosevelt 6 ¢ 32nd US President
**Dwight Eisenhower** 6 / 8 ¢ 34th US President
In 1957, Eisenhower became the first president to travel by helicopter instead of a limo, en route to Camp David (which he had called Shangri-La, but renamed after his grandson).

Benjamin Franklin 7 ¢ Polymath
Albert Einstein 8 ¢ Physicist
Andrew Jackson 10 ¢ 7th US President
Henry Ford 12 ¢ Founder of Ford Motor Company
John F. Kennedy 13 ¢ 35th US President
**Fiorello LaGuardia** 14 ¢ Mayor of New York City in WWII
Read Dick Tracy comics on the radio during a paper strike.

Oliver Wendell Holmes, Jr 15 ¢ Supreme Court Justice
Ernie Pyle 16 ¢ Journalist during World War II
**Elizabeth Blackwell** 18 ¢ First woman to get a medical degree.
After 11 college rejections, male students at Geneva Medical College all voted for her acceptance. They did it as a joke.

George C Marshall 20 ¢ Sec. of State and Sec. of Defense
Amadeo Giannini 21 ¢ Founder of Bank of America
Frederick Douglass 25 ¢ Slavery escapee, abolitionist leader
John Dewey 30 ¢ Educational pioneer
Thomas Paine 40 ¢ Helped inspire the American Revolution
Lucy Stone 50 ¢ Suffragist and slavery campaigner
Eugene O'Neill $1 Playwright
John Bassett Moore $5 Jurist

# Sixties Game Shows

Recovery from the quiz show scandal of the fifties was a gradual process. Big prize money was out; games were in—the sillier the better, or centered around relationships. "Popcorn for the mind," as game show creator Chuck Barris memorably put it.

College Bowl 🎬 (1953-70)
Snap Judgment 🎬 (1967-69)
To Tell The Truth 🏆 (1956-present)
Dough Re Mi 🎬 (1958-60)
Camouflage 🎬 (1961-62 & 1980)
Dream House 🎬 (1968-84)
Say When!! 🏆 (1961-65)
**Let's Make A Deal** 🎬 (1963-present)
The long-time presenter of the show, Monty Hall, gave rise to the eponymous problem: when one door in three hides a prize and you've made your pick, should you change your answer when the host reveals a "zonk" (dud) behind another door? (The counterintuitive answer is yes!)

Your First Impression 🎬 (1962-64)
**Supermarket Sweep** 🏆 (1965-present)
In one of its many comebacks, 1990 episodes of Supermarket Sweep featured monsters roaming the aisles including Frankenstein and Mr. Yuk.

You Don't Say! 🏆 1963-79)
It's Your Bet 🏆 (1969-73)
Yours For A Song 🏆 (1961-63)
Concentration 🎬 (1958-91)
Seven Keys 🎬 (1960-65)
Queen For A Day 🏆 1945-1970)
Password 🎬 (1961-75)
Video Village 🏆 (1960-62)
**Who Do You Trust?** 🎬 (1957-63)
Originally titled, "Do You Trust Your Wife?"
Personality 🏆 (1967-69)
Beat The Odds 🏆 (1961-69)

# Across the Nation

Another decade passes and you're well into adulthood. Were you reading the news, or making it? Here are the national stories that dominated the front pages.

- ✦ Model Cindy Crawford stars in Super Bowl Pepsi commercial
- ✦ North American Free Trade Agreement signed
- ✦ Hurricane Andrew hits the coast
- ✦ Bill Clinton elected president (right)
- ✦ Space Shuttle Endeavor launched
- ✦ Mafia boss John Gotti sentenced to life imprisonment
- ✦ Great Chicago Flood strikes
- ✦ Cartoon Network begins broadcasting
- ✦ Mall of America opens for business
- ✦ TWA declares bankruptcy
- ✦ Riots occur after officers acquitted in Rodney King beating
- ✦ Microsoft releases Windows 3.1
- ✦ Video telephones become available
- ✦ Ross Perot becomes 3rd party nominee for president
- ✦ Four teen girls torture and murder another teen girl
- ✦ Washington Redskins win the Super Bowl
- ✦ Two large earthquakes hit California
- ✦ Ruby Ridge 11-day siege occurs when marshals serve warrant
- ✦ Peekskill meteorite destroys family's car
- ✦ Military leaves the Philippines after a base there for 100 years
- ✦ Bonnie Blair wins gold in 1992 Winter Olympics
- ✦ Three astronauts perform spacewalks at the same time
- ✦ Shipment of rubber ducks falls overboard (they'll float ashore for years)
- ✦ "You can't handle the truth" becomes a catchphrase

*Born this year:*
- ⚢ Singer Selena Gomez
- ⚢ Rapper Cardi B
- ⚢ Journalist Kaitlan Collins

*Joseph Sohm / Shutterstock*

What did, or didn't, pass the lips of the presidential candidates was the talk of the election in 1992. For incumbent President George H. W. Bush, a 1988 pledge—"Read my lips: no new taxes"—was now a liability with voters following mid-term tax rises.

For the Democratic nominee Bill Clinton, above, the incident under the spotlight was more than 20 years old. Asked if he had ever broken international law, Clinton replied that he'd tried marijuana as a student in 1960s England but "I didn't inhale, and I didn't try it again." The ensuing ridicule didn't ultimately damage Clinton, and he was elected with 370 electoral votes to Bush's 168.

# The Biggest Hits When You Were 30...

How many of these big tunes from the year you turned thirty will still strike a chord decades later?

Prince and the
New Power Generation ♪ Diamonds and Pearls
Whitney Houston ♪ I Will Always Love You
Right Said Fred ♪ I'm Too Sexy
Nirvana ♪ Come As You Are
Brooks and Dunn ♪ Boot Scootin' Boogie
Michael Jackson ♪ Remember the Time
Mr. Big ♪ To Be with You
Mary Chapin Carpenter ♪ I Feel Lucky
Boyz II Men ♪ End of the Road
Eric Clapton ♪ Tears in Heaven
Snap! ♪ Rhythm Is a Dancer
Billy Ray Cyrus ♪ Achy Breaky Heart
En Vogue ♪ My Lovin'
(You're Never Gonna Get It)
Guns N' Roses ♪ December Rain
Tom Cochrane ♪ Life Is a Highway
Diamond Rio ♪ Norma Jean Riley
Sophie B. Hawkins ♪ Damn I Wish I Was Your Lover
U2 ♪ One
Mary J. Blige ♪ Real Love
The Heights ♪ How Do You Talk to an Angel
Genesis ♪ I Can't Dance
Red Hot Chili Peppers ♪ Under the Bridge
The Cure ♪ Friday I'm in Love
TLC ♪ Ain't 2 Proud 2 Beg

# ...and the Movies You Saw That Year, Too

From award winners to crowd pleasers, here are the movies that played as your third decade drew to a close.

Unlawful Entry ✎ Kurt Russell, Madeleine Stowe, Ray Liotta
Home Alone 2 ✎ Macaulay Culkin, Joe Pesci, Daniel Stern
My Cousin Vinny ✎ Joe Pesci, Ralph Macchio, Marisa Tomei
Boomerang ✎ Eddie Murphy, Robin Givens, Halle Berry
**Housesitter** ✎ Steve Martin, Goldie Hawn, Dana Delany
**Meg Ryan and Kim Basinger both rejected the role of Gwen.**

Unforgiven ✎ Gene Hackman, Morgan Freeman, Richard Harris
Sister Act ✎ Whoopi Goldberg, Maggie Smith, Harvey Keitel
A League of Their Own ✎ Tom Hanks, Geena Davis, Madonna
Wayne's World ✎ Mike Myers, Dana Carvey, Tia Carrere
The Hand That
Rocks the Cradle ✎ Annabella Sciorra, Rebecca De Mornay
The Mighty Ducks ✎ Emilio Estevez, Joss Ackland, Lane Smith
Scent of a Woman ✎ Al Pacino, Chris O'Donnell, James Rebhorn
Bram Stoker's Dracula ✎ Gary Oldman, Winona Ryder, Anthony Hopkins
The Bodyguard ✎ Kevin Costner, Whitney Houston, Gary Kemp
White Men Can't Jump ✎ Wesley Snipes, Woody Harrelson, Tyra Ferrell
Basic Instinct ✎ Michael Douglas, Sharon Stone, George Dzund
A Few Good Men ✎ Tom Cruise, Jack Nicholson, Demi Moore
Lethal Weapon 3 ✎ Mel Gibson, Danny Glover, Joe Pesci
**Patriot Games** ✎ Harrison Ford, Anne Archer, Patrick Bergin
**This was the first movie allowed to film at the George Bush Center for Intelligence, CIA Headquarters.**

The Last
of the Mohicans ✎ Daniel Day-Lewis, Madeleine Stowe, Jodhi May
Pinocchio ✎ Cam Clarke, Jim Cummings, Jeannie Elias
Under Siege ✎ Steven Seagal, Gary Busey, Tommy Lee Jones
Honey I Blew
Up the Kid ✎ Rick Moranis, Marcia Strassman, Robert Oliveri
Aladdin ✎ Scott Weinger, Robin Williams, Linda Larkin

# Around the House

Sometimes with a fanfare but often by stealth, inventions and innovations transformed the 20th-century household. Here's what arrived between the ages of 10 and 30.

| | |
|---|---|
| 1972 | Garanimal children clothes |
| 1972 | Science calculator |
| 1973 | BIC lighter |
| 1974 | Rubik's Cube |
| 1975 | Betamax video tape machine |
| 1976 | VHS video tape machine |
| 1977 | Coleco Telstar Arcade game system |
| 1978 | Cordless drill |
| 1979 | **Sony Walkman** |

**The Walkman was born when the co-founder of Sony wanted an easier way to listen to opera.**

| | |
|---|---|
| 1980 | Softsoap liquid soap |
| 1981 | IBM Personal Computer |
| 1982 | Ciabatta |
| 1982 | CD Player |
| 1983 | Dyson vacuum cleaner |
| 1984 | Sharp Nintendo Television |
| 1985 | Teddy Ruxpin talking teddy bear |
| 1986 | Atari 7800 game system |
| 1987 | Hooked on Phonics educational materials |
| 1988 | Sega Genesis game system |
| 1989 | Game Boy |
| 1990 | IBM PS/1 computer |
| 1991 | Puzz 3D puzzle |
| 1992 | ThinkPad laptop |

IBM'sThinkPad became the trusted corporate choice and was good enough for NASA, too: a standard-issue laptop was used in space to repair the Hubble telescope.

Here's one that didn't quite make the grade: AT&T's Picturephone, demonstrated here at the 1964 New York World's Fair. A trial set up that year invited the public to rent two of the Picturephone rooms set up in New York, Chicago, and Washington ($16 for 3 minutes). The take-up over the following years was almost nil, but Picturephones went on sale in 1970 anyway with a prediction of a billion-dollar business by 1980. The devices were withdrawn from sale in 1973.

# Female Olympic Gold Medalists in Your Lifetime

These are the women who have stood atop the podium the greatest number of times at the Summer Olympics, whether in individual or team events.

**Jenny Thompson** (8) 🏅 Swimming
Thompson is an anesthesiologist. She started her medical training in 2000—although she took time out while studying to win further gold World Championship medals.

Katie Ledecky (7) 🏅 Swimming
Allyson Felix (7) 🏅 Athletics
Amy Van Dyken (6) 🏅 Swimming
Dana Vollmer (5) 🏅 Swimming
Missy Franklin (5) 🏅 Swimming
Sue Bird (5) 🏅 Basketball
**Diana Taurasi** (5) 🏅 Basketball
The late Kobe Bryant dubbed Taurasi the "white mamba"; for others she is the G.O.A.T. in women's basketball.

Allison Schmitt (4) 🏅 Swimming
Dara Torres (4) 🏅 Swimming
Evelyn Ashford (4) 🏅 Athletics
Janet Evans (4) 🏅 Swimming
Lisa Leslie (4) 🏅 Basketball
Sanya Richards-Ross (4) 🏅 Athletics
Serena Williams (4) 🏅 Tennis
**Simone Biles** (4) 🏅 Gymnastics
Biles's phenomenal medal tally in Olympics and World Championships is greater than any other US gymnast.

Tamika Catchings (4) 🏅 Basketball
Teresa Edwards (4) 🏅 Basketball
Venus Williams (4) 🏅 Tennis

# Toys of the Sixties

The sight, feel and even smell of childhood toys leaves an indelible mark long after they've left our lives. Who can forget that metallic tang of a new Tonka toy, or the *shh-shh* noise as someone erased your masterpiece with a shake of your Etch-a-Sketch?

Chatty Cathy

G.I. Joe

Barbie's Dream House

### Ken

Barbie's boyfriend made an entrance two years after we first met the billion-selling blonde doll. Ken's undewear was welded on in 1971, around the same time he acquired stick-on sideburns. What a guy.

Easy-Bake Oven

SuperBall

Lite-Brite

Hot Wheels

Rock-a-Stack

Chatter Telephone

Etch A Sketch

Thingmaker

Tonka Trucks

### Johnny Seven O.M.A.

One weapon to top them all: 1964's big seller boasted functions that included an anti-tank rocket, grenade launcher and a Tommy gun.

See 'n Say

Barbie

Spirograph

### Frisbee

Fred Morrison didn't invent Frisbees: that honor goes to the first person to discover that a lid is great fun to throw. But Morrison spotted the universal appeal—and the potential to make an affordable plastic version.

Slip 'n Slide

Rock 'Em Sock 'Em Robots

# Drinks of the Sixties

In the cocktail cabinet or behind the bar, these are the drinks your parents' generation were enjoying in the sixties. How many of their choices became yours when you became old enough to enjoy them?

Falstaff beer
**Rusty Nail cocktail**
Rumored to be a favorite drink of the Rat Pack.

Hull's Cream Ale
Stinger cocktail
Rheingold Extra Dry Lager
Gunther's Beer
Lone Star Beer
The Gimlet cocktail
The Grasshopper cocktail
**Little King's Cream Ale**
Best known for its miniature seven-ounce bottles.

Mai Thai cocktail
Genesee Cream Ale
**Storz Beer**
From Nebraska, Storz was "Brewed for the beer pro."

**Iron City Beer**
Iron City is reputed to have introduced the first twist-off bottle cap in 1963.

Golden Dream cocktail
**Mint Julep cocktail**
It's the official drink of the Kentucky Derby, with around 120,000 served over the weekend.

Koch's Light Lager Beer
Arrow 77 Beer
Daiquiri cocktail
Manhattan cocktail
Sterling Premium Pilsner
Carling Black Label
Hamm's Beer
Old fashioned cocktail

# Seventies Game Shows

With enough water under the bridge since the 1950s scandals, producers of seventies game shows injected big money into new formats and revamped favorites, some of them screened five nights a week. How many did you cheer on from the couch?

High Rollers 🏆 (1974–88)

Gambit 🏆 (1972–81)

**The New Treasure Hunt** 🏆 (1973–82)
Perhaps the best-known episode of this show saw a woman faint when she won a Rolls Royce—that she later had to sell in order to pay the taxes.

The Cross-Wits 🏆 (1975–87)

Hollywood Squares 🏆 1966–2004)

**The Newlywed Game** 🏆 (1966–2013)
Show creator Chuck Barris also made "3's a Crowd"— the show in which men, their secretaries and their wives competed. The public wasn't happy.

**Pyramid** 🏆 (1973–present)
Thanks to inflation and rival prizes, the $10,000 Pyramid in 1973 didn't last long: from 1976 it was raised in increments to its current peak of $100,000.

Dealer's Choice 🏆 (1974–75)

Sports Challenge 🏆 (1971–79)

Tattletales 🏆 (1974–84)

It's Your Bet 🏆 (1969–73)

Celebrity Sweepstakes 🏆 (1974–77)

Rhyme and Reason 🏆 (1975–76)

Three On A Match 🏆 (1971–74)

The Match Game 🏆 (1962–present)

Sale of the Century 🏆 (1969–89)

**The Dating Game** 🏆 (1965–99)
The Dating Game—known as Blind Date in many international versions—saw many celebrity appearances before they became well-known, including the Carpenters and Arnold Schwarzenegger.

# Popular Boys' Names

**40**

Just as middle age crept up unnoticed, so the most popular names also evolved. The traditional choices—possibly including yours—are fast losing their appeal to new parents.

Jacob

Michael

**Joshua**

Joshua is very much a turn-of-the-century kind of name. He entered the Top 100 in 1972 and climbed to spend 25 years inside the top 5; now, he rarely makes the top 50.

Matthew

Ethan

Andrew

Joseph

Christopher

Nicholas

Daniel

William

Anthony

David

Tyler

Alexander

Ryan

John

James

Zachary

Brandon

Jonathan

Justin

Dylan

Christian

Samuel

Austin

**Rising and falling stars:**

Dominic, Jaden, Owen, Hayden, Diego and Riley are in; Jared, Garrett, Mark, Jeremy and Bryce are out.

# Popular Girls' Names

It's a similar story for girls' names. Increasing numbers are taking their infant inspiration from popular culture. The worlds of music, film and theater are all fertile hunting grounds for those in need of inspiration.

### Emily

Emily has held the top slot for 12 years since 1900—more than most. Though nobody comes close to Mary (54 years). Others: Linda (6), Lisa (8), Jennifer (15), Jessica (9), Ashley (2), Emma (6), Isabella (2), Sophia (3) and Olivia (since 2019).

Madison
Hannah
Emma
Alexis
Ashley
Abigail
Sarah
Samantha
Olivia
Elizabeth
Alyssa
Lauren
Isabella
Grace
Jessica
Brianna
Taylor
Kayla
Anna
Victoria
Megan
Sydney
Rachel

### Rising and falling stars:

Say hello to Riley, Lily, Ava, Maya and Jocelyn; wave goodbye to Angela, Courtney and Christina.

# NBA Champions Since You Were Born

These are the winners of the NBA Finals in your lifetime—and the number of times they've taken the title.

- **Boston Celtics (13)**
  1966: After the Lakers won Game 1 of the NBA Finals, the Celtics named their star Bill Russell player-coach. He was the first black coach in the NBA. The Celtics responded by winning the series.

- Philadelphia 76ers (2)
- New York Knicks (2)
- Milwaukee Bucks (2)
- **Los Angeles Lakers (12)**
  1980: With Kareem Abdul-Jabbar out with an injury, Lakers' 20-year-old rookie Magic Johnson started at center in the clinching Game 6 and scored 42 points and snared 15 rebounds.

- **Golden State Warriors (4)**
  2015: LeBron James and Stephen Curry, the stars of the teams that faced off in the 2015 NBA Finals, were both born in the same hospital in Akron, Ohio.

- Portland Trail Blazers (1)
- Washington Bullets (1)
- Seattle SuperSonics (1)
- Detroit Pistons (3)
- Chicago Bulls (6)
- Houston Rockets (2)
- San Antonio Spurs (5)
- Miami Heat (3)
- Dallas Mavericks (1)
- Cleveland Cavaliers (1)
- Toronto Raptors (1)

# Fashion in the Seventies

The decade that taste forgot? Or a kickback against the sixties and an explosion of individuality? Skirts got shorter (and longer). Block colors and peasant chic vied with sequins and disco glamor. How many of your seventies outfits would you still wear today?

**Wrap dresses**
Diane von Fürstenberg said she invented the silent, no-zipper wrap dress for one-night stands. "Haven't you ever tried to creep out of the room unnoticed the following morning? I've done that many times."

Tube tops
**Midi skirt**
In 1970, fashion designers began to lower the hemlines on the mini skirt. This change wasn't welcomed by many consumers. Women picketed in New York City with "stop the midi" signs.

Track suit, running shoes, soccer jerseys
Cowl neck sweaters
His & hers matching outfits
Cork-soled platform shoes
Caftans, Kaftans, Kimonos and mummus
Prairie dresses
Cuban heels
Gaucho pants
Chokers and dog collars as necklaces
Birkenstocks
Tennis headbands
Turtleneck shirts
Puffer vests
Long knit vests layered over tops and pants
Military surplus rucksack bags
**"Daisy Dukes" denim shorts**
Daisy's revealing cut-off denim shorts in The Dukes of Hazzard caught the attention of network censors. The answer for actor Catherine Bach? Wear flesh-colored pantyhose—just in case.

Yves Saint Laurent
Shrink tops
Bill Gibb

# Drinks of the Seventies

Breweries were bigger, and there were fewer of them. Beers were lighter. But what could you (or your parents) serve with your seventies fondue? How about a cocktail that's as heavy on the double-entendre as it was on the sloe gin? Or perhaps match the decade's disco theme with a splash of blue curaçao?

**Amber Moon cocktail**
Features an unbroken, raw egg and featured in the film Murder on the Orient Express.

Billy Beer
Rainier Beer
Point Special Lager
Tequila Sunrise cocktail
Regal Select Light Beer
Stroh's rum
Long Island Iced Tea cocktail
Merry Widow cocktail
Shell's City Pilsner Premium Beer
Brass Monkey cocktail
The Godfather cocktail
Brown Derby
Sea-Breeze cocktail

**Schlitz**
This Milwaukee brewery was the country's largest in the late sixties and early seventies. But production problems were followed by a disastrous ad campaign, and by 1981 the original brewery was closed.

Alabama Slammer cocktail
Golden Cadillac cocktail
Harvey Wallbanger cocktail
Red White & Blue Special Lager Beer
Lite Beer from Miller

**Coors Banquet Beer**
A beer that made the most of its initial limited distribution network by floating the idea of contraband Coors. The idea was so successful that Coors smuggling became central to the plot of the movie Smokey and the Bandit.

# US Open Tennis

Across the Open Era and the US National Championship that preceded it, these men won between the year you turned 19 (matching the youngest ever champ, Pete Sampras) and 38 (William Larned's age with his seventh win, in 1911).

| | |
|---|---|
| 1979–81 | John McEnroe |
| 1982–83 | Jimmy Connors |
| 1984 | John McEnroe |
| 1985–87 | Ivan Lendl |

Lendl was the world's number 1 player for 270 weeks during the eighties, though a win at Wimbledon eluded him. His low-key persona earned him the cutting Sports Illustrated headline, "The Champion That Nobody Cares About".

| | |
|---|---|
| 1988 | Mats Wilander |
| 1989 | Boris Becker |
| 1990 | **Pete Sampras** |

19-year-old Sampras became the youngest male player ever to win.

| | |
|---|---|
| 1991–92 | **Stefan Edberg** |

Jimmy Connors made an improbable run to the 1991 US Open Semifinal at age 39. In the 1992 semifinal, Stefan Edberg and Michael Chang played the longest match ever: 5 hours, 26 minutes.

| | |
|---|---|
| 1993 | Pete Sampras |
| 1994 | **Andre Agassi** |

Agassi was the first unseeded champion since Fred Stolle in 1966.

| | |
|---|---|
| 1995–96 | Pete Sampras |
| 1997–98 | Patrick Rafter |
| 1999 | Andre Agassi |
| 2000 | Marat Safin |
| 2001 | Lleyton Hewitt |

# Books of the Decade

Family, friends, TV, and more: there are as many midlife distractions as there are books on the shelf. Did you get drawn in by these bestsellers, all published in your thirties?

| | |
|---|---|
| 1992 | The Bridges of Madison County by Robert James Waller |
| 1992 | The Secret History by Donna Tartt |
| 1993 | The Celestine Prophecy by James Redfield |
| 1993 | Like Water for Chocolate by Laura Esquivel |
| 1994 | The Chamber by John Grisham |
| 1994 | Disclosure by Michael Crichton |
| 1995 | The Horse Whisperer by Nicholas Evans |
| 1995 | The Lost World by Michael Crichton |
| 1995 | The Rainmaker by John Grisham |
| 1996 | Angela's Ashes by Frank McCourt |
| 1996 | Bridget Jones's Diary by Helen Fielding |
| 1996 | Infinite Jest by David Foster Wallace |
| 1997 | American Pastoral by Philip Roth |
| 1997 | Tuesdays with Morrie by Mitch Albom |
| 1998 | The Poisonwood Bible by Barbara Kingsolver |
| 1998 | A Man in Full by Tom Wolfe |
| 1999 | The Testament by John Grisham |
| 1999 | Hannibal by Thomas Harris |
| 1999 | Girl with a Pearl Earring by Tracy Chevalier |
| 2000 | Angels & Demons by Dan Brown |
| 2000 | Interpreter of Maladies by Jhumpa Lahiri |
| 2000 | White Teeth by Zadie Smith |
| 2001 | Life of Pi by Yann Martel |
| 2001 | The Corrections by Jonathan Franzen |

# Supreme Court Justices Since You Were Born

These are the Supreme Court Justices appointed during your lifetime.

| | |
|---|---|
| 1962-93 | Byron White |
| 1967-91 | Thurgood Marshall |
| 1969-86 | Warren E. Burger |
| 1970-94 | Harry Blackmun |
| 1972-87 | Lewis F. Powell Jr. |
| 1972-87 | William Rehnquist |
| 1975-2010 | John Paul Stevens |
| 1981-2006 | Sandra Day O'Connor |
| 1986-2016 | **Antonin Scalia** <br> Known for his strongly worded but often funny opinions, Scalia had nine children. |
| 1988-2018 | Anthony Kennedy |
| 1990-2009 | David Souter |
| 1991- | Clarence Thomas |
| 1993-2020 | **Ruth Bader Ginsburg** <br> RBG was known for wearing lace jabot collars. She had some reserved for issuing majority opinions and other for issuing dissents. |
| 1994- | Stephen Breyer |
| 2005- | John Roberts |
| 2006- | Samuel Alito |
| 2009- | **Sonia Sotomayor** <br> This justice is the first Hispanic member of the Supreme Court. She is a loyal New York Yankees baseball fan. |
| 2010- | Elena Kagan |
| 2017- | Neil Gorsuch |
| 2018- | Brett Kavanaugh |
| 2020- | Amy Coney Barrett |

# The Biggest Hits When You Were 40

Big tunes for a big birthday: how many of them enticed your middle-aged party guests onto the dance floor?

Nickelback 🎙 How You Remind me

Puddle of Mudd 🎙 Blurry

Eminem 🎙 Without Me

The Dixie Chicks 🎙 Long Time Gone

Kylie Minogue 🎙 Can't Get You Out of My Head

LeAnn Rimes 🎙 Can't Fight the Moonlight

Ashanti 🎙 Foolish

Red Hot Chili Peppers 🎙 Can't Stop

Kenny Chesney 🎙 The Good Stuff

Jewel 🎙 Standing Still

3 Doors Down 🎙 When I'm Gone

The Soggy Bottom Boys 🎙 I Am a Man of Constant Sorrow

Nelly featuring Kelly Rowland 🎙 Dilemma

The Calling 🎙 Wherever You Will Go

Rascal Flatts 🎙 I'm Movin' On

Pink 🎙 Don't Let Me Get Me

John Mayer 🎙 No Such Thing

Martina McBride 🎙 Blesses

No Doubt 🎙 Hey Baby

Michelle Branch 🎙 All You Wanted

Creed 🎙 My Sacrifice

Diamond Rio 🎙 Beautiful Mess

Mary J. Blige 🎙 Family Affair

Five for Fighting 🎙 Superman (It's Not Easy)

# Popular Food in the 1970s

From fads to ads, here's a new collection of dinner party dishes and family favorites. This time it's the seventies that's serving up the delights—and some of us are still enjoying them today!

Watergate Salad
Black Forest cake
Chex Mix
Cheese Tid-Bits
Dolly Madison Koo-koos (cupcakes)

**Life Cereal**
"I'm not gonna try it. You try it. Let's get Mikey...he hates everything." Three on- and off-screen brothers, one memorable ad that ran for much of the seventies.

**The Manwich**
"A sandwich is a sandwich, but a manwich is a meal," the ads announced in 1969.

Tomato aspic
Bacardi rum cake
Impossible pies
Zucchini bread
Oscar Mayer bologna
Poke Cake made with Jell-O
Libbyland Dinners

**Reggie! Bar**
Named after New York Yankees' right fielder Reggie Jackson and launched as a novely, Reggie! Bars were on sale for six years.

Hostess Chocodiles
Polynesian chicken salad
Salmon mousse
Cheese log appetizer
Gray Poupon Dijon Mustard

**Tootsie Pop**
So how many licks does it take to get to the center of a Tootsie Pop? 364, and that's official: it was tested on a "licking machine."

# Cars of the 1970s

A decade of strikes, federal regulations, foreign imports, oil crises, safety and quality concerns: car sales were up overall, but the US industry was under pressure like never before. Iconic new models to debut include the Pontiac Firebird and the outrageous, gold-plated Stutz Blackhawk.

| | |
|---|---|
| 1940 | **Chrysler New Yorker**<br>When is a New Yorker not a New Yorker? The eighth generation of this upscale car bore little resemblance to the 1940 launch models. Yet in 1970, the New Yorker was barely middle-aged: they lived on until 1997. |
| 1948 | Ford F-Series |
| 1959 | General Motors Cadillac Coupe de Ville |
| 1959 | Chrysler Plymouth Valiant |
| 1960 | Chrysler Dodge Dart |
| 1961 | **General Motors Oldsmobile Cutlass**<br>The Cutlass outsold any other model in US for four consecutive years, notching up nearly 2 million sales. |
| 1962 | General Motors Chevrolet Nova |
| 1965 | General Motors Chevrolet Caprice |
| 1965 | Ford LTD |
| 1967 | General Motors Pontiac Firebird |
| 1968 | BMW 2002 |
| 1970 | Chrysler Dodge Challenger |
| 1970 | General Motors Chevrolet Monte Carlo |
| 1970 | General Motors Chevrolet Vega |
| 1970 | American Motors Corporation Hornet |
| 1970 | Ford Maverick |
| 1971 | Nissan Datsun 240Z |
| 1971 | **Stutz Blackhawk**<br>These luxury automobiles started at a cool $22,000 ($150,000 today); the first car sold went to Elvis. Among the many other celebrity Blackhawk owners was Dean Martin; one of his three models sported the vanity plate DRUNKY. He crashed it. |
| 1971 | Ford Pinto |
| 1973 | Honda Civic |
| 1975 | Ford Granada |
| 1978 | Ford Fiesta |

# US Banknotes

The cast of US banknotes hasn't changed in your lifetime, giving you plenty of time to get to know them. (Although if you have a lot of pictures of James Madison and Salmon P. Chase around the house, you might want to think about a visit to the bank.)

**Fifty cent paper coin** (1862-1876) 💵 Abraham Lincoln
These bills were known as "shinplasters" because the quality of the paper was so poor that they could be used to bandage leg wounds during the Civil War.

**One dollar bill** (1862-1869) 💵 Salmon P. Chase
The US Secretary of Treasury during Civil War, Salmon P. Chase is credited with putting the phrase "In God we trust" on US currency beginning in 1864.

**One dollar bill** (1869-present) 💵 George Washington
Some bills have a star at the end of the serial number. This means they are replacement bills for those printed with errors.

One silver dollar certificate (1886-96) 💵 Martha Washington
**Two dollar bill** (1862-present) 💵 Thomas Jefferson
Two dollar bills have a reputation of being rare, but there are actually 600 million in circulation in the US.

Five dollar bill (1914-present) 💵 Abraham Lincoln
Ten dollar bill (1914-1929) 💵 Andrew Jackson
Ten dollar bill (1929-present) 💵 Alexander Hamilton
Twenty dollar bill (1865-1869) 💵 Pocahontas
Twenty dollar bill (1914-1929) 💵 Grover Cleveland
Twenty dollar bill (1929-present) 💵 Andrew Jackson
Fifty dollar bill (1914-present) 💵 Ulysses S. Grant
**One hundred dollar bill** (1914-1929) 💵 Benjamin Franklin
The one hundred dollar bill has an expected circulation life of 22.9 years while the one dollar bill has an expected circulation life of just 6.6 years.

Five hundred dollar bill (1918-1928) 💵 John Marshall
Five hundred dollar bill (1945-1969) 💵 William McKinley
One thousand dollar bill (1918-1928) 💵 Alexander Hamilton
One thousand dollar bill (1928-1934) 💵 Grover Cleveland
Five thousand dollar bill (1918-1934) 💵 James Madison
Ten thousand dollar bill (1928-1934) 💵 Salmon P. Chase

# Male Olympic Gold Medalists in Your Lifetime

These are the male athletes that have scooped the greatest number of individual and team gold medals at the Summer Olympics in your lifetime.

Michael Phelps (23) 🥇 Swimming (right)

Carl Lewis (9) 🥇 Athletics

**Mark Spitz (9)** 🥇 Swimming

For 36 years, Spitz's 7-gold-medal haul at the 1972 Munich Olympics was unbeaten; Michael Phelps finally broke the spell with his eighth gold in Beijing.

Matt Biondi (8) 🥇 Swimming

**Caeleb Dressel (7)** 🥇 Swimming

Dressel's epic five gold medals at the 2020 Tokyo Olympics makes him just one of five Americans to have achieved this feat in your lifetime.

Ryan Lochte (6) 🥇 Swimming

Don Schollander (5) 🥇 Swimming

Gary Hall Jr. (5) 🥇 Swimming

Aaron Peirsol (5) 🥇 Swimming

Nathan Adrian (5) 🥇 Swimming

Tom Jager (5) 🥇 Swimming

Greg Louganis (4) 🥇 Diving

Jason Lezak (4) 🥇 Swimming

John Naber (4) 🥇 Swimming

Jon Olsen (4) 🥇 Swimming

Lenny Krayzelburg (4) 🥇 Swimming

Matt Grevers (4) 🥇 Swimming

**Michael Johnson (4)** 🥇 Athletics

Once the fastest man in the world over 200 meters, Johnson took 15 minutes to walk the same distance in 2018 following a mini-stroke—but took it as a sign that he'd make a full recovery.

Between 2000 and 2016, Michael Phelps won 28 Olympic medals, including 23 gold and 16 for individual events. That's 10 more than his nearest competitor, Larisa Latynina, a gymnast of the Soviet Union who took her last gold medal fifty years earlier.

# Winter Olympics Venues Since You Were Born

Unless you're an athlete or winter sports fan, the Winter Olympics can slip past almost unnoticed. These are the venues; can you remember the host countries and years?

Lillehammer
Salt Lake City
Sapporo
**Albertville**
The last Games to be held in the same year as the Summer Olympics, with the next Winter Olympics held two years later.

Turin
Grenoble
Beijing
Sarajevo
Lake Placid
Sochi
**Innsbruck (twice)**
This usually snowy city experienced its mildest winter in 60 years; the army was called in to transport snow and ice from the mountains. Nevertheless, twelve years later, the Winter Olympics were back.

Nagano
Calgary
Vancouver
PyeongChang

# Fashion in the Eighties

Eighties fashion was many things, but subtle wasn't one of them. Influences were everywhere from aerobics to Wall Street, from pop princesses to preppy polo shirts. The result was chaotic, but fun. How many eighties throwbacks still lurk in your closet?

Stirrup pants
Ralph Lauren
Ruffled shirts
Jean Paul Gaultier
**Acid wash jeans**
Stone washing had been around a while, but the acid wash trend came about by chance—Rifle jeans of Italy accidentally tumbled jeans, bleach, and pumice stone with a little water. The result? A fashion craze was born.

Camp collar shirt with horizontal stripes
Thierry Mugler
Oversized denim jackets
Scrunchies
**"Members Only" jackets**
Members Only military-inspired jackets were marketed with the tagline "When you put it on...something happens."

Paper bag waist pants
Pleated stonewash baggy jeans
Cut-off sweatshirts/hoodies
Vivienne Westwood
Azzedine Alaia
Shoulder pads
Dookie chains
Leg warmers
Bally shoes
Jordache jeans
Calvin Klein
Windbreaker jackets
**Ray-Ban Wayfarer sunglasses**
Popularized by Tom Cruise in the movie Risky Business.

Parachute pants
Jumpsuits

# World Buildings

Some of the most striking and significant buildings in the world sprang up when you were between 25 and 50 years old. How many do you know?

| | |
|---|---|
| 1987 | Fuji Xerox Towers, Singapore |
| 1988 | Canterra Tower, Calgary |
| 1989 | The Louvre Pyramid, Paris |
| 1990 | Bank of China Tower, Hong Kong |
| 1991 | One Canada Square, London |
| 1992 | Central Plaza, Hong Kong |
| 1993 | Westendstrasse 1, Frankfurt |
| 1994 | Shinjuku Park Tower, Tokyo |
| 1995 | Republic Plaza, Singapore |
| 1996 | **Petronas Twin Towers, Kuala Lampur** |

1996 **Petronas Twin Towers, Kuala Lampur**
As iconic in Malaysia as the Eiffel Tower is in France. Its skybridge is actually two stories and is the highest of its kind in the world.

| | |
|---|---|
| 1997 | Guggenheim Museum Bilbao |
| 1998 | City of Arts and Sciences, Valencia |
| 1999 | **Burj Al Arab, Dubai** |

1999 **Burj Al Arab, Dubai**
Taller than the Eiffel Tower, this sail-as-a-hotel building does nothing by halves with 17 types of pillow, 16 florists on staff and a helipad that once hosted Andre Agassi and Roger Federer for a stunt tennis match.

| | |
|---|---|
| 2000 | Emirates Tower One, Dubai |
| 2004 | 30 St Mary Axe (The Gherkin), London |
| 2007 | Heydar Aliyev Center, Baku |
| 2008 | Atlantis, The Palm, Dubai |
| 2008 | Fundação Iberê Camargo, Porto Alegre |
| 2010 | Burj Khalifa, Dubai |
| 2011 | Harpa Concert Hall, Reykjavik |
| 2012 | The Shard, London |

# Kentucky Derby Winners

These are the equine and human heroes from the "most exciting two minutes of sport" during your thirties and forties. Did any of them make you rich?

| | |
|---|---|
| 1992 | Lil E. Tee (Pat Day) |
| 1993 | Sea Hero (Jerry Bailey) |
| 1994 | Go for Gin (Chris McCarron) |
| 1995 | Thunder Gulch (Gary Stevens) |
| 1996 | Grindstone (Jerry Bailey) |
| 1997 | Silver Charm (Gary Stevens) |
| 1998 | **Real Quiet (Kent Desormeaux)**<br>Real Quiet missed out on a Triple Crown by fractions of a second. |
| 1999 | Charismatic (Chris Antley) |
| 2000 | Fusaichi Pegasus (Kent Desormeaux) |
| 2001 | Monarchos (Jorge F. Chavez) |
| 2002 | War Emblem (Victor Espinoza) |
| 2003 | Funny Cide (Jose A. Santos) |
| 2004 | **Smarty Jones (Stewart Elliott)**<br>Smarty Jones narrowly avoided losing his eyesight in a 2003 accident; alongside him in the 2004 Derby was the one-eyed horse Pollard's Vision, and Imperialism, a horse with poor vision in his right eye. |
| 2005 | Giacomo (Mike E. Smith) |
| 2006 | Barbaro (Edgar Prado) |
| 2007 | Street Sense (Calvin Borel) |
| 2008 | Big Brown (Kent Desormeaux) |
| 2009 | Mine That Bird (Calvin Borel) |
| 2010 | Super Saver (Calvin Borel) |
| 2011 | Animal Kingdom (John Velazquez) |
| 2012 | I'll Have Another (Mario Gutierrez) |

# World Series Champions Since You Were Born

These are the winners of the Commissioner's Trophy and the number of times they've been victorious in your lifetime.

- ⚾ Detroit Tigers (2)
- ⚾ New York Yankees (7)
- ⚾ Cincinnati Reds (3)
- ⚾ St. Louis Cardinals (5)
- ⚾ **Los Angeles Dodgers (5)**
  1988: Dodgers' Kirk Gibson, battling injuries, hit a game-winning home run in his only at-bat of the 1988 World Series.
- ⚾ Pittsburgh Pirates (2)
- ⚾ Baltimore Orioles (3)
- ⚾ **New York Mets (2)**
  1969: The Mets had never finished above 9th in their division.
- ⚾ Oakland Athletics (4)
- ⚾ Philadelphia Phillies (2)
- ⚾ Kansas City Royals (2)
- ⚾ **Minnesota Twins (2)**
  1991: Both teams had finished in last place the previous season.
- ⚾ Toronto Blue Jays (2)
- ⚾ Atlanta Braves (2)
- ⚾ Florida Marlins (2)
- ⚾ Arizona Diamondbacks (1)
- ⚾ Anaheim Angels (1)
- ⚾ Boston Red Sox (4)
- ⚾ Chicago White Sox (1)
- ⚾ San Francisco Giants (3)
- ⚾ **Chicago Cubs (1)**
  2016: The Cubs' first World Series win since 1908.
- ⚾ Houston Astros (1)
- ⚾ Washington Nationals (1)

# Books of the Decade

By our forties, most of us have decided what we like to read. But occasionally a book can break the spell, revealing the delights of other genres. Did any of these newly published books do that for you?

| | |
|---|---|
| 2002 | Everything is Illuminated by Jonathan Safran Foer |
| 2002 | The Lovely Bones by Alice Sebold |
| 2003 | The Da Vinci Code by Dan Brown |
| 2003 | The Kite Runner by Khaled Hosseini |
| 2004 | The Five People You Meet in Heaven by Mitch Albom |
| 2004 | Cloud Atlas by David Mitchell |
| 2005 | Never Let Me Go by Kazuo Ishiguro |
| 2005 | The Book Thief by Markus Zusak |
| 2005 | Twilight by Stephanie Meyer |
| 2006 | The Secret by Rhonda Byrne |
| 2006 | Eat, Pray, Love by Elizabeth Gilbert |
| 2006 | The Road by Cormac McCarthy |
| 2007 | A Thousand Splendid Suns by Khaled Hosseini |
| 2007 | City of Bones by Cassandra Clare |
| 2008 | The Hunger Games by Suzanne Collins |
| 2008 | The Girl with the Dragon Tattoo by Stieg Larsson |
| 2009 | Catching Fire by Suzanne Collins |
| 2009 | The Lost Symbol by Dan Brown |
| 2009 | The Help by Kathryn Stockett |
| 2010 | The Girl Who Kicked the Hornets' Nest by Stieg Larsson |
| 2010 | Mockingjay by Suzanne Collins |
| 2010 | Freedom by Jonathan Franzen |
| 2011 | Fifty Shades of Grey by E.L. James |
| 2011 | The Best of Me by Nicholas Sparks |
| 2011 | Divergent by Veronica Roth |

# Vice Presidents in Your Lifetime

The linchpin of a successful presidency, the best springboard to become POTUS, or both? Here are the men—and woman—who have shadowed the most powerful person in the world in your lifetime.

| | |
|---|---|
| 1961-63 | Lyndon B. Johnson |
| 1965-69 | **Hubert Humphrey**<br>Christmas 1977: with just weeks to live, the former VP to President Johnson made goodbye calls. One was to Richard Nixon, the man who had beaten Humphrey to become president in 1968. Sensing Nixon's unhappiness at his status as Washington outcast, Humphrey invited him to take a place of honor at a funeral he knew was fast approaching. |
| 1969-73 | **Spiro Agnew (right)** |
| 1973-74 | Gerald Ford |
| 1974-77 | Nelson Rockefeller |
| 1977-81 | Walter Mondale |
| 1981-89 | **George H. W. Bush**<br>He is only the second vice president to win the presidency while holding the office of vice president. |
| 1989-93 | **Dan Quayle**<br>Quayle famously misspelled potato ("potatoe") |
| 1993-2001 | **Al Gore**<br>This VP won the Nobel Peace Prize in 2007, following in the footsteps of two other former vice presidents. |
| 2001-09 | Dick Cheney |
| 2009-17 | Joe Biden |
| 2017-20 | **Mike Pence**<br>In the 90s, Pence took a break from politics to become a conservative radio talk show and television host. |
| 2020- | Kamala Harris |

Spiro Agnew resigned in 1973, the second VP to quit in America's history (the first was John Calhoun in 1932). He stepped down after being charged with tax evasion and taking bribes. He covered his legal debts with a loan from friend Frank Sinatra. In 1983 he was compelled to repay $268,000: the money he had taken in bribes, plus interest.

# British Prime Ministers in Your Lifetime

These are the occupants of 10 Downing Street, London, during your lifetime (not including Larry the resident cat). Don't be deceived by that unassuming black (blast-proof) door: Number 10 was originally three houses and features a warren of more than 100 rooms.

| | |
|---|---|
| 1957–63 | **Harold Macmillan** |

**Harold Macmillan**
Macmillan was the scion of a wealthy publishing family. He resigned following a scandal in which a minister was found to have lied about his relationship with a 19-year-old model. Macmillan died aged 92; his last words were, "I think I will go to sleep now."

| | |
|---|---|
| 1963–64 | Sir Alec Douglas-Home |
| 1964–70 | Harold Wilson |
| 1970–74 | Edward Heath |
| 1974–76 | Harold Wilson |
| 1976–79 | James Callaghan |
| 1979–90 | **Margaret Thatcher** |

**Margaret Thatcher**
In 1994, Thatcher was working late in a Brighton hotel, preparing a conference speech. A bomb—planted weeks earlier by the IRA five stories above—detonated, devastating the hotel. Five were killed; Thatcher was unscathed. The conference went ahead.

| | |
|---|---|
| 1990–97 | John Major |
| 1997–2007 | Tony Blair |
| 2007–10 | **Gordon Brown** |

**Gordon Brown**
Brown has no sight in his left eye after being kicked in a school rugby game; in 2009, while Prime Minister, rips in the right retina were also diagnosed.

| | |
|---|---|
| 2010–16 | David Cameron |
| 2016–19 | **Theresa May** |

**Theresa May**
Asked in a pre-election interview about the naughtiest thing she'd ever done, May said that she'd once run through a field of wheat with her friends, and that the farmers "weren't too happy".

| | |
|---|---|
| 2019– | Boris Johnson |

# Things People Do Now (Part 2)

Imagine your ten-year-old self being given this list of today's mundane tasks and habits—and the puzzled look on your face!

+ Listen to a podcast
+ Go "viral" or become social media famous
+ Watch YouTube
+ Track the exact location of family members via your smartphone
+ Watch college football playoffs
+ Have drive-thru fast food delivered to your door
+ Check reviews before trying a new restaurant or product
+ Use LED light bulbs to save on your electric bill
+ Wear leggings as pants for any occasion
+ Use hashtags (#) to express an idea or show support
+ Join a CrossFit gym
+ Use a Forever stamp to send a letter
+ Carry a reusable water bottle
+ Work for a company with an "unlimited" paid time off policy
+ "Binge" a TV show
+ Marry a person of the same sex
+ Take your shoes off when going through airport security
+ Take a selfie
+ Use tooth-whitening strips
+ Feed babies and kids from food pouches
+ Buy recreational marijuana from a dispensary (in some states)
+ Store documents "in the cloud" and work on them from any device
+ Clean up after your pets using compostable waste bags
+ Buy free-range eggs and meat at the grocery store

# A Lifetime of Technology

It's easy to lose sight of the breadth and volume of life-enhancing technology that became commonplace during the 20th Century. Here are some of the most notable advances to be made in the years you've been an adult.

| | |
|---|---|
| 1983 | Internet |
| 1986 | Mir Space Station |
| 1988 | **Internet virus** |
| | The first Internet worm was specifically designed to crack passwords. Its inventor was the son of the man who invented computer passwords. |
| 1989 | World Wide Web |
| 1992 | Digital hand-sized mobile phone |
| 1995 | **Mouse with scroll wheel** |
| | Mouse scroll wheels were developed primarily as a zoom function for large Excel sheets, but became more useable as a means of scrolling. |
| 1996 | DVD player |
| 1997 | WebTV |
| 1998 | Google |
| 1999 | Wi-Fi |
| 2000 | Camera phone |
| 2001 | Wikipedia |
| 2004 | Facebook |
| 2005 | **Google Maps** |
| | Google used solar-powered cameras attached to sheep to map the Faroe Islands for Street View, or Sheep View as it became known. |
| 2006 | Twitter |
| 2007 | Apple iPhone |
| 2007 | Amazon Kindle |
| 2009 | Bitcoin |
| 2012 | **Tesla's Model S** |
| | It has taken 150 years of refinement, but battery-powered cars are here: and Tesla's Model S was among the first to show it is possible, practical and desirable. |
| 2013 | Large Hadron Collider |
| 2014 | Amazon Alexa |

# US Open Tennis

And now it's the women's turn. Here are the tournament's victors when you were between the ages of the current "winning window": 16 years (Tracy Austin in 1979), and a venerable 42 years (Molla Mallory in 1926: she won eight times).

| | |
|---|---|
| 1975-78 | **Chris Evert**<br>During the 1975 US Open, Evert beat her long-time rival Martina Navratilova in the semi-final. That evening, Navratilova defected to the United States. |
| 1979 | Tracy Austin |
| 1980 | Chris Evert |
| 1981 | Tracy Austin |
| 1982 | Chris Evert |
| 1983-84 | Martina Navratilova |
| 1985 | Hana Mandikova |
| 1986-87 | **Martina Navratilova**<br>The four US Open finalists in 1986 (two male, two female) were all born in Czechoslovakia. |
| 1988-89 | Steffi Graf<br>Gabriela Sabatini |
| 1991-92 | Monica Seles |
| 1993 | Steffi Graf |
| 1994 | Arantxa Sanchez Vicario |
| 1995-96 | Steffi Graf |
| 1997 | **Martina Hingis**<br>16-year-old Hingis defeated 17-year-old Venus Williams in the youngest Grand Slam tournament final of the Open era. |
| 1998 | Lindsay Davenport |
| 1999 | Serena Williams |
| 2000-01 | **Venus Williams**<br>Venus beat her sister Serena in the 2001 final. |
| 2002 | Serena Williams |
| 2003 | Justine Henin |
| 2004 | Svetlana Kuznetsova |

# Grand Constructions

Governments around the world spent much of the 20th century nation building (and rebuilding), with huge civil engineering projects employing new construction techniques. Here are some of the biggest built between the ages of 25 and 50.

| | |
|---|---|
| 1987 | Pikeville Cut-Through, US |
| 1988 | Great Seto Bridge, Japan |
| 1989 | Skybridge (TransLink), Canada |
| 1990 | Ningbo Lishe International Airport, China |
| 1991 | Fannefjord Tunnel, Norway |
| 1992 | Vidyasagar Setu Bridge, India |
| 1993 | Rainbow Bridge, Japan |
| 1994 | **English Channel tunnel, UK & France**<br>Even at its predicted cost of $7 billion, the longest underwater tunnel in the world was already the most expensive project ever. By the time it opened, the bill was more than $13 billion. |
| 1995 | Denver International Airport, US |
| 1996 | Tenerife International Centre for Trade Fairs and Congresses, Spain |
| 1997 | British Library, UK |
| 1998 | SuperTerminal 1, Hong Kong |
| 1999 | **Northstar Island, US**<br>Northstar is a five-acre artificial island created off Prudhoe Bay, Alaska. Pack ice means a conventional floating platform can't be used; during construction, an ice road brought in supplies. |
| 2000 | Hangzhou Xiaoshan International Airport, China |
| 2004 | **Millau Viaduct, France**<br>The world's tallest bridge at 336m, the viaduct carries road traffic 270m above the valley floor. |
| 2012 | Three Gorges Dam, Yangtze River, China |
| 2028? | **Brenner Base Tunnel (between Italy and Austria)**<br>Due to be the second longest railway tunnel in the world on completion, at a cost of around US$10 billion. |

# Popular Food in the 1980s

The showy eighties brought us food to dazzle and delight.
Food to make us feel good, food to share and food to go.
Some innovations fell by the wayside, but many more can
still be found in our baskets forty years later.

### Hot Pockets

Hot Pockets were the brainchild of two brothers, originally
from Iran. Their invention was launched as the Tastywich before
being tweaked to become the Hot Pockets enjoyed by millions.

Bagel Bites
Crystal Light
Steak-Umms
Sizzlean Bacon
Potato skins appetizers
Tofutti ice cream

### Hi-C Ecto Cooler

Hi-C has been around for a very long time, but the Ecto Cooler
dates back to the Ghostbusters movie hype of the 1980s.

Hot buttered O's
Knorr Spinach Dip
Original New York Seltzer
Blondies

### Blackened Redfish

The trend for blackening redfish prompted fish stocks
to drop so low that commercial fishing for the species
was banned in Louisiana.

Bartles & Jaymes Wine Coolers
Fruit Wrinkles
Stuffed mushrooms appetizers

### TCBY Frozen Yogurt

TCBY originally stood for "This Can't Be Yogurt."

Sushi
Fajitas
Capri Sun
Jell-O Pudding Pops

### Lean Cuisine frozen meals

Lean Cuisine is an FDA-regulated term, so all
Lean Cuisine frozen meals need to be within
the limit for saturated fat and cholesterol.

# Eighties Symbols of Success

In the flamboyant era of Dallas and Dynasty there were many ways to show that you, too, had really made it. Forty years on, it's fascinating to see how some of these throwbacks are outdated or available to nearly everyone, while others are still reserved for today's wealthy peacocks.

BMW car

Cellular car phone

Rolex watch

**Cosmetic surgery**

In 1981 there were 1,000 liposuction procedures performed. That number increased to 250,000 by 1989.

VCR

"Home theater" projection TV

In-ground pool

AKC-registered dog

McMansion

Pagers/"beeper"

Aprica stroller

Home intercom system

Heart-shaped Jacuzzi tub

**NordicTrack**

This machine was originally called the Nordic Jock but was renamed due to compaints from women's rights groups.

Cruise vacation

**Restaurant-standard kitchen appliances**

A popular commercial stove produced enough heat to warm an average three-bedroom home. It was the energy equivalent of six residential stoves.

Ronald Reagan-style crystal jelly bean jar on your desk

Apple or Commodore 64 home computer

Volvo Station Wagon

Gordon Gekko-style "power suit"

Owning a horse or riding lessons for your children

Private jet

Tennis bracelet

Monogrammed clothes and accessories

Launched in 1980, the Apple III personal computer seen here went on sale for a hefty $4,000 and up, the equivalent of over $13,000 today. It didn't sell well and was soon withdrawn (unlike the Apple II, which went on to sell more than 5 million units).

# The Transportation Coils

This novel issue of more than 50 definitive stamps first appeared on post in the early eighties, and became a favorite of collectors for its mono color engraved images of transportation methods past and present. Stamps carrying the printing plate number are particularly treasured. Here's a selection you may remember.

1 c 🖾 Omnibus
2 c 🖾 Locomotive
3 c 🖾 Handcar
4 c 🖾 **Stagecoach**
Coaches have been ferrying people and mail between US towns and cities since the late 18th century.

5 c 🖾 Motorcycle
5.5c 🖾 **Star Route Truck**
Star routes were 19th century mail routes on which carriers bid to make deliveries.

6 c 🖾 Tricycle
7.4 c 🖾 Baby Buggy
10 c 🖾 Canal Boat
11 c 🖾 Caboose
12.5 c 🖾 Pushcart
13 c 🖾 Patrol Wagon
15 c 🖾 Tugboat
17 c 🖾 Electric Auto
17 c 🖾 Dog Sled
17.5 c 🖾 Racing car
18 c 🖾 Surrey
20 c 🖾 Cog Railway
21 c 🖾 Railway Mail Car
23 c 🖾 Lunch Wagon
24.1 c 🖾 Tandem Bike
25 c 🖾 Bread Wagon
32 c 🖾 Ferry Boat
$1 🖾 **Sea Plane**
The US Navy bought its first sea plane in 1911: a Curtiss Model E, with a range of 150 miles.

# Eighties Game Shows

By the eighties, game shows had their work cut out to compete against the popularity of new drama and talk shows. Still, an injection of celebrity glamour and dollar bills—alongside hours to be filled on new cable TV channels—ensured their survival. Here are the biggies.

Double Dare 🏆 (1986-2019)
Remote Control 🏆 (1987-90)
Scrabble 🏆 (1984-93)
**The Price Is Right** 🏆 (1972-present)
"Come on down!"—perhaps the best-known game show catchphrase of all time. One 2008 contestant was even happier than usual to do just that after 3 chips dropped into the Plinko all hit the $10,000 jackpot. Fluke? No, wires used to rig the result when filming ads hadn't been removed. She was allowed to keep the $30,000.

Family Feud 🏆 (1976-present)
**Press Your Luck** 🏆 (1983-86)
A show perhaps best remembered for the contestant Michael Larson, who memorized the game board and engineered a winning streak worth over $110,000. It wasn't cheating—Larson kept the winnings—but the game was swiftly reformulated.

Chain Reaction 🏆 1980-present)
Blockbusters 🏆 (1980-87)
Win, Lose, or Draw 🏆 (1987-90)
On The Spot 🏆 (1984-88)
Jeopardy! 🏆 (1964-present)
Card Sharks 🏆 (1978-present)
**Wheel of Fortune** 🏆 (1975-present)
Hostess Vanna White is estimated to clap 600 times a show; that's around 4,000,000 times since she began in 1982.

Fandango 🏆 (1983-88)
Body Language 🏆 (1984-86)
Jackpot! 🏆 (1974-90)

# Game Show Hosts of the Seventies and Eighties

Here is the new generation of hosts: bow-tied, wide-smiled men to steer family favorites through tumultuous times. Astonishingly, one or two are still holding the cards.

John Charles Daly ➤◆ What's My Line (1950–1967)
Garry Moore ➤◆ To Tell The Truth (1969–1976)
Chuck Woolery ➤◆ Love Connection (1983–1994)
Bob Barker ➤◆ The Price Is Right (1972–2007)
**Pat Sajak** ➤◆ Wheel of Fortune (1981–)
Sajak took the crown for the longest-reigning game-show host of all time in 1983, when his 35-year reign surpassed that of Bob Barker as host of The Price is Right.

Peter Tomarken ➤◆ Press Your Luck (1983–86)
Gene Rayburn ➤◆ The Match Game (1962–1981)
**Alex Trebek** ➤◆ Jeopardy! (1984–2020)
At the time of his death in 2020, Trebek had hosted more than 8,200 episodes of the show.

Dick Clark ➤◆ Pyramid (1973–1988)
Richard Dawson ➤◆ Family Feud (1976–1995)
Peter Marshall ➤◆ Hollywood Squares (1966–1981)
Howard Cosell ➤◆ Battle of the Network Stars (1976–1988)
Marc Summers ➤◆ Double Dare (1986–1993)
Tom Kennedy ➤◆ Name That Tune (1974–1981)
Bert Convy ➤◆ Tattletales (1974–78; 1982–84)
Ken Ober ➤◆ Remote Control (1987–1990)
Jim Lange ➤◆ The Dating Game (1965–1980)
Wink Martindale ➤◆ Tic-Tac-Dough (1978–1985)
**Art Fleming** ➤◆ Jeopardy! (1964–1975; 1978–79)
Host for the original version, Fleming declined to host the comeback in 1983. His friend Pat Sajak took the job.

Jack Narz ➤◆ Concentration (1973–78)
Dennis James ➤◆ The Price Is Right (1972–77)
Jim Perry ➤◆ $ale of the Century (1983–89)
John Davidson ➤◆ Hollywood Squares (1986–89)
Ray Combs ➤◆ Family Feud (1988–1994)
Mike Adamle ➤◆ American Gladiators (1989–1996)

# TV News Anchors of the Seventies and Eighties

The explosion in cable channels that began with CNN in 1980 brought a host of fresh presenters to join the ranks of trusted personalities that bring us the news. How many of them do you remember?

**Dan Rather** ♟ (CBS)
"Kenneth, what's the frequency?" Those were the words of the man who attacked Rather in 1986. It took a decade before the message was decoded; his assailant wanted to block the beams he believed TV networks were using to target him.

Peter Jennings ♟ (ABC)
Tom Brokaw ♟ (NBC)
Ted Koppel ♟ (ABC)
Bill Beutel ♟ (ABC)
Jessica Savitch ♟ (NBC)
Connie Chung ♟ (NBC)
Diane Sawyer ♟ (CBS/ABC)
Sam Donaldson ♟ (ABC)
**Barbara Walters** ♟ (ABC)
Walters was a popular pioneer; the first woman to co-host and anchor news programs, reaching 74 million viewers with her interview of Monica Lewinsky.

Frank Reynolds ♟ (ABC)
Jane Pauley ♟ (NBC)
Roger Grimsby ♟ (ABC)
Roger Mudd ♟ (CBS/NBC)
Garrick Utley ♟ (NBC)
Bernard Shaw ♟ (CNN)
Frank McGee ♟ (NBC)
Ed Bradley ♟ (CBS)
Larry King ♟ (CNN)
Kathleen Sullivan ♟ (ABC/CBS/NBC)
Jim Lehrer ♟ (PBS)
**Robert MacNeil** ♟ (PBS)
In 1963, MacNeil had a brief exchange of words with a man leaving the Texas School Book Depository; to this day, it is uncertain whether this was Lee Harvey Oswald.

# FIFA World Cup: Down to the Last Four in Your Life

Here are the teams that have made the last four of the world's most watched sporting event in your lifetime (last year in brackets). The US men's team has reached the semifinals once, back in 1930.

France ⚽ (2018, winner)
**Croatia** ⚽ (2018, runner-up)
During a 2006 match against Australia, Croatian player Josip Šimunić was booked three times due to a referee blunder.

Belgium ⚽ (2018, 3rd)
**England** ⚽ (2018, 4th)
In the run-up to the 1966 World Cup the trophy was stolen and held to ransom. An undercover detective met the crook with fake banknotes and he was arrested; a dog named Pickles found the trophy under a bush.

Brazil ⚽ (2014, 4th)
Germany ⚽ (2014, winner)
Argentina ⚽ (2014, runner-up)
Netherlands ⚽ (2014, 3rd)
Spain ⚽ (2010, winner)
Uruguay ⚽ (2010, 4th)
Italy ⚽ (2006, winner)
Portugal ⚽ (2006, 4th)
Turkey ⚽ (2002, 3rd)
Korean Republic ⚽ (2002, 4th)
Sweden ⚽ (1994, 3rd)
Bulgaria ⚽ (1994, 4th)
Poland ⚽ (1982, 3rd)
Russia ⚽ (1966, 4th)
Czech Republic (as Czechoslovakia) ⚽ (1962, runner-up)
**Chile** ⚽ (1962, 3rd)
The 1962 World Cup saw the 'Battle of Santiago' between Chile and Italy. The first foul occurred 12 seconds into the game, a player was punched in the nose, and police intervened several times.

Serbia (as Yugoslavia) ⚽ (1962, 4th)

# Books of the Decade

Our final decade of books are the bookstore favorites from your fifties (so far!). How many did you read…and can you remember the plot, or the cover?

| | |
|---|---|
| 2012 | Gone Girl by Gillian Flynn |
| 2012 | Me Before You by Jojo Moyes |
| 2013 | The Tenth of December by George Saunders |
| 2013 | Inferno by Dan Brown |
| 2014 | All the Light We Cannot See by Anthony Doerr |
| 2014 | The Goldfinch by Donna Tartt |
| 2015 | The Girl on the Train by Paula Hawkins |
| 2015 | The Nightingale by Kristin Hannah |
| 2016 | Hillbilly Elegy: A Memoir of a Family and Culture in Crisis by J. D. Vance |
| 2016 | Before the Fall by Noah Hawley |
| 2016 | Fool Me Once by Harlan Coben |
| 2017 | Sing, Unburied, Sing by Jesmyn Ward |
| 2017 | Little Fires Everywhere by Celeste Ng |
| 2017 | Eleanor Oliphant is Completely Fine by Gail Honeyman |
| 2018 | Where the Crawdads Sing by Delia Owens |
| 2018 | Normal People by Sally Rooney |
| 2018 | The Tattooist of Auschwitz by Heather Morris |
| 2019 | The Silent Patient by Alex Michaelides |
| 2019 | Daisy Jones & The Six by Taylor Jenkins Reid |
| 2019 | Such a Fun Age by Kiley Reid |
| 2020 | The Midnight Library by Matt Haig |
| 2020 | The Invisible Life of Addie LaRue by V. E. Schwab |
| 2020 | American Dirt by Jeanine Cummins |
| 2021 | The Four Winds by Kristin Hannah |
| 2021 | The Lost Apothecary by Sarah Penner |
| 2021 | The Wife Upstairs by Rachel Hawkins |

April 17, 1970: Jim Lovell is brought aboard a helicopter—the last of the three astronauts from the Apollo 13 mission to be lifted from the floating Command Module.

# Apollo Astronauts

Whatever your personal memories of the events, the moon landings are now woven into our national story—but not all of the Apollo astronauts who made the journey are equally well known. Twelve landed; twelve remained in lunar orbit. Gus Grissom, Ed White, and Roger B Chaffee died in training.

*Landed on the moon:*

Alan Bean

**Alan Shepard**

Shepard was the oldest person to walk on the moon at age 47.

Buzz Aldrin

Charles Duke

David Scott

Edgar Mitchell

Eugene Cernan

Harrison Schmitt

James Irwin

John Young

Neil Armstrong

Pete Conrad

*Remained in low orbit:*

Al Worden

**Bill Anders**

Anders took the iconic "Earthrise" photo.

Dick Gordon

Frank Borman

Fred Haise

Jack Swigert

Jim Lovell

Ken Mattingly

Michael Collins

**Ron Evans**

Made the final spacewalk of the program to retrieve film cassettes.

**Stuart Roosa**

On the Apollo 14 mission he carried seeds from 5 species of trees. They were planted across the US and are known as "Moon Trees."

Tom Stafford

# Things People Did When You Were Growing Up (Part 2)

Finally, here are more of the things we did and errands we ran as kids that nobody needs, wants, or even understands how to do in the modern age!

+ Buy cigarettes for your parents at the corner store as a child
+ Use a pay phone (there was one on almost every corner)
+ Join a bowling league
+ Collect cigarette or baseball trading cards
+ Get frozen meals delivered to your door by the iconic refrigerated yellow Schwan's truck
+ Attend "Lawn Faiths"/ ice cream socials
+ Chat with strangers over CB radio
+ Look up a phone number in the Yellow or White Pages
+ Visit the Bookmobile for new library books
+ Have a radio repaired at an appliance/electronics shop
+ Ride your bike without a helmet
+ Go to American Bandstand parties
+ Take part in a panty raid prank
+ Attend a sock hop
+ Get milk delivered to your door
+ Hang out with friends at a pizzeria
+ Use a rotary phone at home
+ Use a typewriter
+ Save your term paper on a floppy disc
+ Listen to LPs and the newest 45s
+ Care for a pet rock
+ Use a card catalogue to find books at the library
+ Attend a Sadie Hawkins Dance where girls invited the boys
+ Go disco roller skating

Made in the USA
Monee, IL
28 October 2022